Children in the Cradle of Television

About the Author

Edward L. Palmer is professor and chair of the psychology department at Davidson College. He has been a guest researcher at Harvard University's Center for Research in Children's Television and a visiting scholar at UCLA. With Aimee Dorr he coedited a work entitled *Children and the Faces of Television: Teaching, Violence, Selling,* which has become a prominent academic resource and reference. An active researcher in the field of children's television, his focus has centered upon questions relating to program/commercial separation, fright reaction, and comprehension of nutritional information. His research work is frequently cited in professional publications and journals. An invited contributor to the *Wiley Encyclopedia of Psychology,* he has served as a consultant to various groups, including the Council on Children, Media and Merchandising. He was a nominee for the Television and Social Policy Task Force of the American Psychological Association and a member of the Telecommunications Task Force at Rutgers University. He has conducted editorial reviews for several professional journals and the National Science Foundation and is a member of Phi Beta Kappa and various professional organizations.

Children in the Cradle of Television

Edward L. Palmer
Davidson College

Lexington Books
D.C. Heath and Company/Lexington, Massachusetts/Toronto

Library of Congress Cataloging-in-Publication Data

Palmer, Edward L.
  Children in the cradle of television.

  Bibliography: p.
  Includes index.
  1. Television programs for children—United States. I. Title.
PN1992.8.C46P34   1987   791.44'5   85-45317
ISBN 0-669-11299-2 (alk. paper)

Published simultaneously in Canada
Printed in the United States of America
Casebound International Standard Book Number: 0-669-11299-2
Library of Congress Catalog Card Number: 85-45317

The paper used in this publication meets the minimum requirements of American National Standard for Information Sciences—Permanence of Paper for Printed Library Materials, ANSI Z39.48-1984.

87 88 89 90 8 7 6 5 4 3 2 1

To my devoted mother and dad, Eva and Leon, who believed in me and gave me the strength to believe as well.

To Aimee Dorr, who saw potential in this idea spark and provided insights and the opportunity for that spark to mature and grow.

To my family and friends, who shared my enthusiasm, my long days, and my hopes.

To my teachers, students, and colleagues, who brought inspiration to my midst and curiosity to my task.

To Frisky, who never read a book, but knows worlds about accepting me as I am.

Contents

Acknowledgments

A s I think of this project I am deeply aware of the many who helped to bring it to fruition. Without a delicately interwoven team it never could have happened. The idea for this book originated when I was on sabbatical as a visiting scholar at UCLA. Professor Aimee Dorr graciously provided a richly intellectual sabbatical setting, and through her efforts and those of her chairman, Dean John Hawkins, I was welcomed to the Department of Education and its resources. As Aimee and I discussed our research, her insights sparked my own initiative, and Los Angeles provided the optimal setting for doing the research. Two of her doctoral students—Cathy Doubleday and Peter Kovaric—gave painstaking effort and time to the basic interview formats, making recommendations that dramatically improved them.

The network executives and producers whom I interviewed for part II gave generously of their time and perspectives. They included the following. At ABC: Susan Futterman, Vice President, Broadcast Standards; Jennie Trias, Director, Children's Programming. At CBS: Paul Bogrow, Vice President, Hollywood Program Practices, at the time of the interview, and currently Executive Producer, *CBS Storybreak;* Judy Price, Vice President, Children's Programming. At NBC: Maurice Goodman, Vice President, Broadcast Standards, West Coast; Phyllis Tucker Vinson, Vice President, Children's Programming; Winifred White, Director, Children's Programming; Lynn Condon, Professional Staff, Broadcast Standards. At Hanna-Barbera: Joseph Barbera, Chief Executive; Jean MacCurdy, Vice President, Current Programs; Arthur Scott, Vice President, Special Projects; Joseph Taritero, Vice President, Creative Affairs. At Filmation: Lou Scheimer, President/Executive Producer; Arthur Nadel, Executive Vice President, Production; Robert London, Executive Story Editor. At DIC: Andrew Heyward, Chief Executive. At Krofft: Martin Krofft, Chief Executive. At Marvel: Margaret Loesch, President/Chief Executive Officer. At Ruby-Spears: Joseph Ruby, Chief Executive/Executive Producer; Michael Hack, Associate Producer. And at TMS: Sagiko Tsuneda, Chief Executive; Sidney Iwanter, Vice President, Creative Productions; Nicholas Bostedo, Executive Producer.

The Davidson College support staff was equally generous in its time and assistance. On one of her first days on the job, Sarah Davis transcribed an exceptionally lengthy interview, wondering what she had gotten herself into at her new post. Chapters 1 through 4 relied heavily on extensive microfilm research, most of which meant securing the materials through interlibrary loan. Hazel Goodman, Senior Reference Assistant, served as my mainstay throughout those long research months. She ordered materials as I needed them and scouted alternative sources when the original orders did not materialize. She patiently changed the paper roll in the microfilm printer, permitting the work to go on even when it meant considerable inconvenience in her own work day. Cindy Pendergraft, Serials and Documents Head, bypassed a downed microfilm printer by converting a microfiche printer to microfilm. Mary Beaty, Reference Coordinator and Assistant Director of the library, was incredibly supportive as specific reference needs arose. Jane Biggerstaff, Louis Connor, and Benita Peace ran the duplicating/trimming/computer races to the finish line. There would have been no finish line without the assistance of Doug Honeycutt in transferring the book to the administrative computer when the academic one was down for several days. Beth Covington and John Savarese supported and coached me daily through unfamiliar straits. Leland Park, Director of the library, was exceptionally helpful in the copyediting stage. Fern Duncan, Departmental Secretary, patiently read the manuscript and gave tremendously helpful support and feedback.

The daily expressions of interest from friends and colleagues meant so much to me and kept momentum going even when my tired eyes and back wished to quit. That entire community of support reminds me of the William James quote that greets those who enter James Hall at Harvard: "The community stagnates without the impulse of the individual. The impulse dies away without the sympathy of the community." To all who have brought me a beautifully supportive community I am very deeply grateful. A special word of thanks goes to Vola-Claire Espe, Martha Ringer, Duane Hickling, and Dale Van Dalsem, who, in their special ways, challenged me to balance the intensity of research pursuit with weekend ventures into the "California state of mind," the beauty of its peaks and its shores.

Funding support for this project was received from the Faculty Study and Research Committee of Davidson College. Two Academic Vice Presidents, T.C. Price Zimmermann and Robert C. Williams, have been exceptionally supportive in their roles as Committee chair.

Introduction

Birth is a time of exuberance, development, frustration, and needs, and television's birth was all of these. Though preceded by experimentation and technology, the birthplace of commercial television itself was the 1940s. It was the best of times and the worst of times—a decade begun with the hardships and sacrifices of World War II and ended with a baby boom and fertile new markets for consumer goods.

The babies born during this time would be the first generation to rock in the cradle of television. They would live, grow, and develop in commercial television's most spectacular era. Its personalities and its stars would become their daily friends and role models, and its magnetic appeal would be lasting. There would eventually be fear that the TV cradle had rocked too long and too hard, and the baby may have toppled out and been hurt. But that was in the future. In the 1940s, commercial television was an infant that slept most of the day and was not particularly spectacular or creative at night. So much a child itself, television had neither the time nor capacity to think about child viewers. It was developing in the way infants characteristically do, with its own needs very much at the center of things.

Technology and Early Programming

Television's first needs were technological ones. Mechanical scanning in the 1920s had distinct limitations, and it took electronic scanning advances in the 1930s to pave the way for the future. The advances seemed quite promising by 1939 when NBC inaugurated television service at the New York World's Fair, and President Franklin D. Roosevelt, major league baseball games, and college football shared the distinction of being among the first telecasts. World's Fair momentum carried impressively into 1940 as NBC conducted the first network television broadcast—a modest affair between New York and Schenectady—and July

1941 brought the Federal Communications Commission's (FCC) inauguration of commercial television broadcasting (WNBT, New York). Television was progressing dramatically, but so was the specter of war, and in less than six months Pearl Harbor would reverberate through the United States, mobilizing it for defense.[1, 2] Television would need to sleep yet a while longer.

And sleep it did. While radio scheduled feverishly on the hour and half-hour throughout the days and evenings, television in the early 1940s slept on. It would awaken sporadically for a ball game perhaps, or a newsreel, but then it would promptly go back to sleep. There was little reason for it to stay awake for long intervals. Radio was entertaining and informative, and everyone listened to it regularly. Television lacked the resources to stay awake throughout the day and evening. For all kinds of reasons—some vested, some technological, some programming—it was radio's era and a formative time for television.

A five-year-old in the early 1940s would have had little reason to be enthralled with television. Unless a child could summon enthusiasm for film shorts, war news, or sports events, there was no incentive to channel visit. There was the fascination of television's newness, but little more. Although weekday schedules were sleepy at best, Saturday mornings were the sleepiest times of all. The assumption was that parents, aunts, uncles, cousins, and even children slept in on Saturday mornings, so television slept in too. On those rare Saturday mornings when TV awakened, the programming was strictly for adults, with topics such as civil defense and Red Cross training.[3]

During television's slow growth in the 1940s, the basics of future growth and development were actively underway. Few would have imagined that January 1, 1945, when television awakened for only two hours, would be the same day that signaled the year of full-fledged major network television (NBC), a twenty-inch screen (DuMont Laboratories), and the image orthicon camera (RCA). When Germany and Japan surrendered, television via film was there. Its arrival in a general programming context would not be far behind.[4]

The Marketing and Growth Dilemma

Programming takes resources, and resources take revenue, a circular dilemma for a struggling newcomer. After World War II, radio still had broad appeal. Almost everyone had radio receivers, and people such as Edward R. Murrow became legends for their radio coverage of the war. To gain any semblance of status comparable to radio, television would have to surmount several hurdles. The technology hurdle was now behind it due to electron scanning and further refinements that came with the war effort. Programming was another matter. Television needed to be fascinating to attract viewers, and attracting viewers meant creating a viable market of television purchasers. It boiled down to a "sending–receiving" problem. A family found little justification for buying a set if there was nothing interesting to watch, and programming was an expensive proposition with little incentive when the purchasing market had not yet reached significant proportions. Both sides of this equation needed balance.

Imagine yourself as a television set dealer in small quarters on the downtown street corner. For each prospective customer who came into your store you would proudly turn on the latest set—to a test pattern! From the time you opened in the morning until the time you closed at night, most of your customer demonstrations featured only a test pattern. You and your salespeople were caught in the dilemma of having to sell a product that was not yet there. Even in the postwar era of economic boom, there was a limit as to how many sets could be sold on the promise of future programming. Both to create a market and to sustain one, television programming needed to span more of the day. Where you as a set owner would have been one-household-in-a-hundred in 1947, you were one-in-ten by 1950. And the next ten years would bring sets to nine out of ten households, with virtually every U.S. household having one television by 1970. Station revenues of over $100 million in 1950 would catapult to $1.2 billion by 1960. A golden goose was taking wing.[5]

To skyrocket from one-in-a-hundred households to one-in-ten in the narrow space of three years takes far more than selling test patterns. It takes programming. Although a radio leftovers flavor lingered in many TV programs, notable exceptions were beginning to develop television's own identity and build a vastly expanding audience. As programming moved toward all day, set sales mushroomed. By 1948, the nation's television set dealers had sold one million units. Not bad when you have been selling test patterns! Many bought sets for the chance to see NBC's "Texaco Star Theater" with Milton Berle. It was a landslide success and ushered in the variety show format that soon would include Sid Caesar and Imogene Coco, "The Ed Sullivan Show," and several others. Few could resist "I Love Lucy," and the greatest challenge to television-set-holdouts still lay ahead—Bob Smith's "Howdy Doody" at 5:30 on weekday evenings. "Kukla, Fran, and Ollie" was on at 7:00 P.M. followed by "The Lone Ranger" at 7:30.[6] Television's programming appeal to families was strengthening.

Perceived Role and Purpose

When television's first full programming day came in October 1948, the late September announcement gave clear outlines of how families and child viewers would be considered. The announcement also carried profound implications for television's role as a commercial medium, as a babysitter, and as an educator. As "the first video outlet to offer a full schedule of daytime programs on a regular basis," WABD, New York, planned to program for "the whole family at breakfast time and the housewife for the remainder of the day." Commander Mortimer W. Loewi, executive assistant to the president of Allen B. DuMont Laboratories, Inc., indicated the station's awareness that a housewife could not spend her day watching television and at the same time cook, clean, answer the phone and care for children.

> Therefore, our programs will be built in this manner: There will always be something of interest on the screen for those who have the leisure to watch, however the audio part of the program will give the listener the complete story. When viewing becomes necessary as for some outstanding event, an audio signal will cue the listener to watch the screen. As outlined by DuMont officials, the schedule has been designed to coincide with the average housewife's routine. When the housewife has to wash the breakfast dishes or fix luncheon, for instance, there will be programs designed to keep preschool children occupied and out of her way. . . . The station further plans to demonstrate department store products, with the housewife being able to order the merchandise by telephone after she has seen it on the video screen.[7]

Loewi and DuMont scarcely could have realized how profoundly they were speaking about what television was to be. They assumed an all-day audience of housewives with very busy housework schedules, and in effect they were saying, "We know you're busy, and we don't want to interrupt your schedules, but we want you to get our message. We also know those young'uns will be in your hair at dishtimes and mealtimes, and we'll babysit them for you." It was an early suggestion that television would serve as a babysitter. And, like radio before it, there was a clear indication that a major new merchandising medium was starting to bloom.

Implicit Role Assumptions

This seemingly straightforward announcement of Loewi had several tacit assumptions about the viewing audience, family roles, programming, and media selling. It assumed that families would watch television in the early morning and women would be the potential viewers during most of the day. The announcement silently assumed that men were employed outside the home while women remained at home with the children. It also assumed that part of TV's role would be to entertain those children, fascinating them enough to keep them out of mom's hair when she was busy. Perhaps most importantly, the announcement assumed that TV's role in family life and mom's workday would not be an intrusive one. Entertain? Yes! Intrude? No! It might well become the impossible dream, yet the intent was there. Television was growing in the entertainment ways of radio and was learning those marketing skills as well. Whether or not it would be called intrusion, time spent with television would be destined to increase steadily and swiftly. Television would find an eager and receptive audience.

Role of the Child

At this point child viewers were not a commercial market for television. There was not a conscious effort to program and merchandise to them in a direct sense. There was, however, a child focus in the effort to market television sets to families. Perhaps similar to some computer-marketing approaches today, the central thrust of many ads was how much the family—and explicitly the children—would benefit from the TV medium. The ads implied prosocial and educational benefits for child viewers, creating the message that it would be good for the family to have a set.

The scene of the children's future marketplace was still undiscovered. Virtually nothing could stir television cameras to life on Saturday mornings. Television executives wanted to make cost-effective use of their expensive camera equipment, considering it a tremendous extravagance to let it sit idle. But even in this realm of economics, the equipment was very much idle at weekend's dawn. Saturday morning was the notably dark and quiet time of the week, just as it had been in the early 1940s. It was perceived as having no viewers, no marketability, no potential.[8]

DuMont Laboratories and Commander Loewi had set the stage for commercial television when they first announced all-day programming. They already had a concept of their audience and the role of children within it, and they already knew that TV would be similar to the commercial mold of radio. It is doubtful that they knew how strong the mold would be and how compelling.

As we move through the decades of commercial television we will spotlight key features within each era, relating them specifically to child viewers and to Saturday morning programming. Nothing stands in isolation from its environment, and television is no exception. Entertainer, persuader, seller, friend—it has interacted constantly with the depth and richness of its milieu. To grow in a competitive marketplace posed no small challenge for the 1950s, but the power of television would be discovered quite early and the times would prove friendly to the challenge. Television provided fantasy escape with spectacular programming and the allure of the new. Violent upheaval in the 1960s raised profound questions about a fever-ridden nation and the elements contributing to its fever. Was television sick? Had it infected its children? The 1970s brought television issues to a head as advertising and violent programming found themselves in the legal process. The spotlight was on children, and the impact of such diverse elements as *The Surgeon General's Report on Television and Social Behavior*[9], an advertising rule making, "family viewing time," and a prime-time access ruling will be discussed. The issues were basic and reached to the core of First Amendment considerations in a powerful, commercially driven medium.

The 1980s brought an era of deregulation that has challenged and undercut several initiatives from the 1970s. The ten-year follow-up[10] to the Surgeon General's Report confirmed the original document's findings and provided critical analysis of an active television research era. Conservative religious groups attacked commercial television and introduced a disturbing new ideological activism challenging First Amendment freedoms. Sex and violence in programming came under the activists' attacks. Again, as in the past, children have been at the center of the programming controversy. This book will provide information on the producers, network programming, and standards executives who wrestle daily with questions on children's programming, how it comes to be, and its potentials.

References

1. Erik A. Barnouw, *A Tower in Babel—A History of Broadcasting in the United States* (New York: Oxford University Press, 1966).
2. Erik A. Barnouw, *The Golden Web—A History of Broadcasting in the United States*, Vol. 2 (New York: Oxford University Press, 1968).
3. *New York Times* (January 1, 1942), p. L 51.
4. *New York Times* (January 1, 1945), p. L 29.
5. C.H. Sterling and T.R. Haight, *The Mass Media: Aspen Institute Guide to Communication Industry Trends* (New York: Praeger, 1978).
6. *New York Times* (September 25, 1949), p. 12 X.
7. WABD (New York, September 21, 1948).
8. *New York Times* (September 21, 1948), p. L 54.
9. Surgeon General's Scientific Advisory Committee on Television and Social Behavior. *Television and Growing Up: The Impact of Televised Violence*. Report to the Surgeon General, United States Public Health Service. Washington, D.C.: U.S. Government Printing Office, 1972.
10. David Pearl, *Television and Behavior: Ten Years of Scientific Progress and Implications for the Eighties: Volume 1, Summary Report* (Rockville, Md.: U.S. Department of Health and Human Services, National Institute of Mental Health, 1982), pp. iii–viii, 1–8.

Part I
The Historical Landscape

1
The Golden Age of Programming

T elevision in the 1950s would later be recalled with a hint of wistfulness, great admiration, and affection. "It Was New and We Were Very Innocent" said John Crosby, famed TV critic, in the title for his recollections of that decade.[1] One could walk into a bar and find the customers excitedly discussing the previous night's drama on "Playhouse 90." "Kukla, Fran, and Ollie" was fascinating inquisitive adults and children alike, and television became a training ground for both Broadway and the movies. In Crosby's words, "Talent seemed to gush right out of the cement."[2] Its actors and actresses, stars, and comedians were giants. Its humor was innocent, without the honesty and "bite" that soon would follow. Both grown-ups and children found it spectacular.

Wide-eyed family members who had watched little or no television at the dawn of the fifties broke the five-hour-a-day viewing mark by a minute in 1956. A new lifestyle was taking root, and within it a nation was welcoming a household guest of incredible power and influence.

An Age of Fear

Beneath a veneer of peacefulness, the general landscape was troubled. Russia exploded an atomic bomb in August 1949, causing a collective shudder throughout the United States. Now for the first time in history two superpowers had entered the nuclear age. The United States as well as the rest of the world were living in the shadow of the bomb. Responses to the Russian development were as troublesome as the development itself. Some began to question how a backward country such as Russia could have bridged the technological gap so rapidly, and this questioning was fueled by allegations that physicists in the Manhattan Project had been pipelining technical information to Russian intelligence. Anti-Communist hysteria swept the nation, and Julius and Ethel Rosenberg were executed. They were the first Americans to be executed for espionage during peacetime.

The times were ripe for a "red hunt," and Senator Joseph R. McCarthy, chairman of the Senate Permanent Subcommittee on Investigations, mounted his emotional, anti-Communist campaign. His style was tailormade for television, and we will see how he skillfully used TV to fan emotional fires in the populace. Capitalizing on Communist fear and hysteria, McCarthy campaigned to remove from State Department libraries any books alleged to be written by Communists or their "fellow travelers." It seemed easy to be included in one of McCarthy's lists, and as he would tour the country to expose "twenty years of treason" (p. 519) of the Democratic Party, he would regularly pull out a list before crowds to further fan the emotional fires he already had created. It was occurrences such as these in the McCarthy era that prompted President Eisenhower to admonish Dartmouth graduates, in June 1953, not to join the book burners. Eisenhower knew the deadly effectiveness with which McCarthy was manipulating and building on a nation's fears. Fear, red hunts, and arms escalation in a nuclear age were creating an unsettled time.[3]

Amid the intense U.S. anti-Communist hysteria, at home, the Korean War was raging abroad. Termed a "patrol action" by President Truman, it claimed 39,000 American lives before the Korean armistice was signed on June 27, 1953. With the end of the Korean conflict the focus of unrest would change from abroad to the home front. Paratroopers that once might have anticipated a Korean destination soon were dispatched to Little Rock, Arkansas, as President Eisenhower mobilized the Arkansas National Guard to ensure the enrollment of blacks at Little Rock's Central High School. The prelude to this event came on May 17, 1954, when the Supreme Court in *Brown* v. *Board of Education of Topeka* reversed an 1896 ruling allowing "separate but equal" educational facilities for blacks. On May 31, 1955, the Supreme Court ordered lower courts to use "all deliberate speed" in admitting black children to public schools. The pace of events quickened as Rosa Parks refused to move to the back of the bus and blacks boycotted the segregated city bus lines in Montgomery, Alabama. Dr. Martin Luther King, Jr. led the movement to further challenge segregation in restaurants, stores, theaters, and other public places. The conflict at home had been enjoined, and like the Korean conflict before it, this initiative would not be without its pain, trials, loss, and blood.

Perhaps not insignificantly, this era brought with it the birth of the tranquilizer. Miltown first appeared in 1950 and others soon would follow, scoring record profits for the drug industry. In another medical breakthrough, the nation would witness its largest immunization test in history as Dr. Jonas E. Salk began vaccinating elementary school pupils in 1954 with his newly developed antipoliomyelitis vaccine. Although the events of the decade had spawned many fears, the long-standing fear of polio was coming to an end.

To have television be new, spectacular, and innocent in an age of fear, gave it the role of Camelot in a troubled environment. People could turn to TV to escape, and they could accomplish this escape in their homes. Movie theaters, an earlier escape route, now felt threatened and attempted three-dimensional technology with special eyeglasses to compete. Although short-lived, the approach soon led to the development of CinemaScope, the wide-screen, stereophonic sound format that was adopted by virtually every theater in the country.[4] The race was on to compete with this young television giant who demonstrated remarkable capacities and strengths as a powerful persuader, a family friend, and a magnificent marketer.

Powerful Persuader

Politicians were quick to discover television's unique ability to tap emotions and affect attitudes. Three events from the 1950s—the 1952 presidential campaign, its "Checkers" drama, and the televised Army-McCarthy hearings—demonstrated this power.

For the first time ever a presidential campaign was airing visually in living rooms and kitchens throughout the United States in 1952, and the TV planning was ingenious. Eisenhower's headquarters had engaged the services of an advertising firm called Batten, Barton, Durstine & Osborn to plan strategy and orchestrate media details of his campaign appearances. Here for the first time a candidate and a campaign were becoming a television production. An Eisenhower speech for a thirty-minute program was to be no more than twenty minutes long. The remaining ten minutes would be devoted to a carefully planned arrival and departure of the hero. The careful study of the hall, the placement of cameras, and the planned scene-by-scene coverage resembled a well-crafted television script. In shot-by-shot planning, Barnouw recounted one such staging in the campaign. A paraphrase of the script reads like this:

> Ike entering through back door of the auditorium; Ike greeting crowd; crowd going wild, craning necks to see him; Ike being escorted down the aisle; Mamie in box seat; Ike stepping up on platform; crowd going wild; Ike standing at rostrum, waving; Ike looking toward Mamie; Mamie smiling; Ike on cue holding up arms to stop applause; and [recurrent script theme] crowd going wild.

Political appearances such as these were very skillfully planned and fine-tuned. Campaigns and their candidates in the television age would never again be the same. Showmanship and scripting had taken on a vital new dimension. We were entering an era where the success or failure of political candidates rode on how well they were packaged and scripted for TV.

The "Checkers" speech from the 1952 campaign demonstrated yet another dimension of television's power—the power to tug at heartstrings. Eisenhower's political image had a clean, national-hero aura, and he had gone on record as stating that his campaign must be "clean as a hound's tooth." In light of that image and commitment, it was no small embarrassment when rumors surfaced that running-mate Nixon allegedly funneled some California-based political campaign funds for personal use. There were calls for him to withdraw as Eisenhower's running mate, and Nixon went into seclusion to develop his televised response. The appearance was as skillfully scripted as the campaign had been. Pat Nixon sat at her husband's side, and in the opening scene viewers were introduced to her. During the program Nixon would turn to Pat on occasion, and the cameras would closely focus on her. Most heart-rending of all was the confession of the personal gift the Nixons had received during the campaign. Hushed viewers all across the country heard the story of the man in Texas who had learned of their daughter's wish for a dog. In dramatic and emotional terms, Nixon described the arrival of a package at Union Station in Baltimore and its precious cargo—a black and white spotted cocker spaniel puppy. He told of six-year-old Tricia naming it Checkers, how much they loved it, and their desire to keep it. There was hardly a dry eye anywhere among viewers, and the power of the presentation could be sensed instantaneously. Even as Nixon concluded the telecast with his request that viewers send their opinions to the Republican National Committee, one already knew that the response would be one of overwhelming support. The spotted cocker spaniel stayed with the Nixons, and Nixon stayed on the Republican ticket.[5] In one of the earliest dramas of the 1950s television era, a political candidate had found direct access to a nation's emotions. Checkers had become television's early canine success story, soon to be rivaled by the likes of Lassie and Rin Tin Tin.

Senator Joseph McCarthy found television equally effective in tapping a nation's fears and suspicions. Communist mania already was rampant in the media and in the public consciousness. Magazine articles bore titles such as "How Communists Get That Way," "Trained to Raise Hell in America," "Reds Are After Your Child," and "How Communists Take Over." Mickey Spillane's 1951 thriller, *One Lonely Night,* sold over three million copies. In Spillane's book the hero, Mike Hammer, bragged that he had pumped slugs into "the nastiest bunch of bastards you ever saw." Hammer's maligned group, the Communists, also were called "red sons-of-bitches" who figured Americans were all "soft as horse manure and just as stupid."[6] To have the elevation of "horse manure" in the midst of this descriptive menagerie seemed almost anachronistic, but the key point was the nature of the media setting and the nature of Mike Hammer. As Joseph McCarthy moved from Wisconsin obscurity to the television limelight, it was almost as though Spillane's Mike Hammer had come vividly to life. What followed was one of the most persuasive and masterful television dramas of fear and suspicion ever to be aired. McCarthy would be a television ratings draw consistently from 1950 to 1955, and within his wake he would build existing communist mania to peaks of the irrational and the hysterical. Television cameras followed their new star with an intensity that would have been the envy of any political candidate. From Wheeling to Salt Lake City to

Reno to the floor of the Senate, McCarthy and his charges of lists of avowed Communists were carried and continually repeated. The mania-ridden public watched, and the popularity of McCarthy grew. Attracting support from influential Catholics and fundamentalists alike, he became a superpatriot to some while others even termed him a religious savior. All of this popularity, and the television coverage that fostered it, brought McCarthy considerable and insidious power.

Prime time in the McCarthy television drama came in the form of the 1954 Army-McCarthy Senate hearings. From April 22 through June 17, the televised hearings were a national sensation. Here for the first time millions of American viewers witnessed the raw, venomlike attacks their devoted red hunter would make on virtually anyone including the Army's top brass. The tide of his popularity began to turn, giving the Senate the courage to investigate and to register a condemnation vote in December 1954.[7] For nearly five years a senator from Wisconsin had preyed on a nation's fears, and had built a vast, intimidating, cultlike following. The slander from the McCarthy era carried innumerable and deep scars for many innocent individuals, and tragically wrecked reputations. As McCarthy moved toward discredit and disgrace, the populace seeds that had brought him to power lingered. Although television in the final analysis had led to his downfall, television also had elevated him to the hero position he had held among the mass audience. The power of the medium and the ability of an individual to manipulate national fears to tragic ends was a television reality that needed to remain vivid in the nation's memory.

Family Friend

The fears of the fifties had spawned several social complexions. Conformity, a quiet generation of college students, and a focus on family and middle-class values were basic to this complexion, and the family became central to television's programming. In many ways the programming era of the late 1950s seemed closely akin to the McCarthy era and Checkers. Values and morals were defined in black and white, clear-cut terms. Heroes and villains were easy to distinguish. It was a time of moral simplicity and absolutes. It was also a time of fantasy, the spectacular, and family values.

As homes increasingly welcomed television, personalities like Howdy and Tommy Rettig (Lassie's faithful keeper) became like members of the family. A kind of media intimacy was developing in which events in the lives of beloved television characters held the emotional significance of events in one's own family. If Tommy Rettig had fallen and broken his leg, for instance, the news likely would have eclipsed superpower summits, hydrogen bomb testing, and other lead stories of the day. Program-based personalities were loved and treasured in millions of homes across the United States, and there were many program characters who shared this favored status. Buffalo Bob and Howdy were sacred to young viewers, as were Kukla, Fran, Ollie and Smilin' Ed's Gang. There were Paul Winchell and his lovable dummy, Jerry Mahoney, along with Roy Rogers, Hopalong Cassidy, the Lone Ranger, Uncle Johnny Coons, Gene Autry, and Captain Kangaroo. Reflecting its radio heritage, television had a vast, male-dominated array of hosts and stars to befriend and entertain children. There were also child actors like Jeff and Timmy on "Lassie"—stars the same age as their viewers so young children could identify with them.

Puppetry was plentiful in the late 1950s. "Howdy Doody" and "Kukla, Fran, and Ollie" ranked high along with "Beany and Cecil," "Lucky Pup," "Rootie Tootie/Kazootie," and "Captain Kangaroo's" stable of puppet friends. And for every success there were scores of little-knowns—the Shirley Swines, the Blinkys, and the Uncle Mistletoes. Besides puppets, the prominent format was live-action adventure, mostly westerns. "The adventures of" were far and away the most prevalent words found in program listings. Cyclone Malone, Kit Carson, Jim Bowie, Long John Silver, Robin Hood, Superman, and even Pow Wow were among the many who were set to have adventures. Although puppet friends and live-action adventure covered the vast majority of what children were seeing, circuses also were gaining popularity.[8] By comparison with these formats, cartoons were still in their infancy. Cartoon animation had come to television (for example, Pow Wow, and Heckle and Jeckle), but it was not yet the dominant format. The late 1950s were beginning to signal the onset of the children's cartoon era, and that era would sweep past puppetry and live action with phenomenal speed and staying power.

Why did puppetry and live action fade? Probably the single most direct factor was the advent of animation techniques which made cartoon production cost effective for television. Cartoons of the 1950s were generally transplants from the movies, and there was very little incentive to make cartoons for television. Full animation was prohibitively expensive, and it would take the pioneering genius of Hanna-Barbera to scale that hurdle through partial animation and camera moves. The animators of the film industry were not predisposed to consider television production, because television was the enemy that threatened to empty movie theaters. While many film animators were searching for choice epithets, Disney had come to television. That grand entrance and the development of partial animation techniques paved the way for the sweep of the 1960s. Television would soon discover that it could earn greater profit margins with cartoons than with other types of children's programming. Meanwhile, some of the greats among puppet/live-action adventure had run their course in the 1950s. Ed McConnell had died, Bob Smith had a heart attack, and networks were discovering that their weekday time slots were more profitable with adult programming. "Howdy Doody" was relegated to Saturday mornings—not synonymous with Alcatraz, but surely unwelcome news to any who had been in the weekday spotlight. A similar fate would befall others later—a "Captain," for instance.

Magnificent Marketer

In 1931, Felix had observed that "Advertising will be ready for the visual medium long before the visual medium is ready for advertising."[9] The comment could not have been more strikingly prophetic for children as they became a television market. Initially children had been of interest to marketers as a means of selling television sets to families, but now as nine out of ten households acquired sets, that interest changed. Times that once had been programmed for children now were more profitable with adult programming, and the once diverse time schedules of children's programs began to shrink from weekdays and concentrate on Saturday mornings. For years, Saturday morning had been the problem stepchild of the programming week. It could be filled with public service and low priority entries, but networks generally had perceived it as the cost-inefficient time to program. Why program? Who would watch?

At a time when networks were looking to expand their markets, an answer to the Saturday morning question was unfolding. Why not relocate those children's shows that had lost their weekday slots? If anyone would watch TV on Saturday mornings, children were the likely candidates. It was worth a try. NBC began testing the Saturday morning waters in 1951 and 1952 as it moved "Kukla, Fran, and Ollie," and considered the merits of transferring other shows such as "Lucky Pup," "Tom Corbett," "Ranger Joe," and "Magic Cottage." CBS tested more seriously in 1953 as it slated "Rod Brown of the Rocket Rangers," "Big Top," "Sky King," and "The Lone Ranger" for the Saturday morning plunge. By 1954, there was even talk of "Operation Saturday" (NBC), as though it was a major offensive in the network battleship formation. With children's shows concentrated in the Saturday time period, networks had a very attractive marketing message to their prospective advertisers. This was the advertiser's chance to communicate with children.[10]

The sales lessons television had picked up from radio were learned well by Saturday morning programmers. Network competition, ratings, and counter-programming became well seasoned on weekends. The program flow typically moved from other time slots toward Saturday morning. In some instances, the "transplant's" success had come from the movies (for example, "Woody Woodpecker", and in other cases, a prime-time program would transplant to Saturday morning animation after it had run its course (for example, "Circus Boy"). This pattern would become more common in the sixties and seventies. But the most familiar pattern was one-season stands by a cadre of Saturday morning program hopefuls that failed to make their ratings. Few people can recall "Acrobat Ranch," "Bobo the Hobo," or "Barnyardville Varieties." These shows appeared briefly on Saturday mornings and disappeared. There were exceptions, and a handful of them reached well beyond the hurdle of one year's network airing.[11]

Where children's programming had once sold television sets, the sets now sold products to children through program advertising. On host shows the host routinely advertised and promoted products to young viewers. In fact, the sponsor's name sometimes became the name of the main character as it did in the case of "Captain Hartz."[12] "Romper Room" had one of the most direct merchandising approaches. With a combination of syndicated and locally based program elements, it promoted and sold a diverse line of "Romper Room" products ranging from toys to moccasins. As we will see later, it took several more years before these selling techniques would formally come into question.

Interestingly, one of the most ingenious marketing techniques took place on one of the most impressive new program series for children. After premiering in October 1954, Walt Disney aired an elaborate, multifaceted series in 1955 that included Tomorrowland (space adventures), Fantasyland (Mickey Mouse and the entire Disney cast of animated characters), Frontierland (the legends, heroes, and folklore of America), and Adventureland (ventures around the world within the animal kingdom). This was the most diverse, comprehensive approach to children's programming yet to be aired, and we see within it the promotional seeds and themes of the now famous Disneyland and Disneyworld.[13] It was an ingenious use of the programming medium as a marvelous sales promotion tool for future enterprises.

By now there was strong evidence that network competition and counterprogramming were coming to children's schedules. In 1955—the year of Disney and the "Mickey Mouse Club"—CBS was prompted to add four adventure serials (one being "Sergeant Preston of the Yukon") and a weekday morning show for two- to eight-year-olds called "Captain Kangaroo." The dean of child storytellers since the 1930s was Smilin' Ed McConnell, a radio favorite who had transplanted to television in the twilight of his beloved twenty-eight years with children. Smilin' Ed's death in 1954 and Andy Devine's succession left their popular show open to the "Captain Kangaroo" competition. The Captain, Bob Keeshan, was more than equal to the challenge. He had studied with Bob Smith, Howdy, and Clarabell the clown, and he knew the television ropes as well as he knew children. Smilin' Ed McConnell, Buffalo Bob, and Howdy raced against Captain Kangaroo. A torch was passing and the Captain was the youngest runner. "Captain Kangaroo" emerged as a victor in the competition of counterprogramming, but eventually he, too, would become a victim of the marketplace realities.

For children's programming in a competitive environment there were bellwethers of what lay ahead. "Howdy Doody" headed from weekday to Saturday status in June 1956. Adult shows were more profitable in weekday time slots, and network interest in preschool programming was correspondingly diminishing. Children's Westerns were experiencing a similar trend as network interest in adult Westerns began to vaporize the guitar-toting cowboys. "Howdy Doody's" tenth birthday at the end of 1957 was an occasion of mixed emotions. The show's success and growth had far exceeded expectations. Howdy's birthday show was number 2,200! Buffalo Bob Smith emceed the occasion with a "This is Your Life" type program that included Clarabell, Dilly Dally,

Phineas T. Bluster, Buffalo Bob and his ingenius producer Roger Muir. The decline of "Howdy Doody" and other children's shows was still faint, but would become much more distinct in the 1960s.[14]

Concern for Children . . . on a Quiet Note

Concern about children's programming and television's impact on young viewers grew in the 1960s and 1970s but it was even present in the idyllic programming environment of the 1950s. Given the upbeat, spectacular nature of the programming era, the concerns remained in isolated pockets rather than in general groundswell proportion. As we observe later, it is hard to generate support for child-issue concerns on a sunny day, and this was television programming's successful era. Nonetheless, a significant number of parents, psychologists, and educators were raising questions about TV role models and the effects of TV viewing on children.

Concern had surfaced early in the 1950s when the National Association of Educational Broadcasters (NAEB) examined the prevalence of crime and horror programming in commercial television schedules. Surveying four television markets in major cities, NAEB found these programs accounting for ten percent of the schedule day. This thread of public concern continued through 1954 when Senator Estes Kefauver's subcommittee examined the causes of juvenile delinquency. High on the subcommittee's list of culpable parties was crime/violence programming in commercial television, and its 1956 report stated that television violence could be potentially harmful to young viewers. On the basis of its inquiry and findings, the Kefauver Committee urged commercial broadcasters to reduce crime/violence programming. But the market momentum took priority, and subsequent surveys by the subcommittee in 1961 and 1964 revealed a notable increase in the prevalence of television violence.[15] Commercial markets were ripe for harvesting, and the yield from violent programming was high. The subcommittee and its concerns were clearly running against the tide.

As the underworld character was made a star, as the stupid husband image was glorified, as wrestling and roller derby became major television sports, people wondered and worried . . . and watched. The almost magnetic appeal of TV, and the amount of time children spent watching it, were among the most prominent concerns. There were the bizarre but true news stories like the eleven-year-old girl in Galesburg, Illinois, whose grandmother had compelled her to turn off the television during a thunderstorm. Because of television deprivation she went berserk, slapped her grandmother, stabbed her ten-year-old brother with a pair of scissors, and attacked her mother with a butcher knife.[16] Although the news story itself was related half-tongue-in-cheek, it articulated a deep and underlying concern about this new and magnetic medium.

What was it doing to children, and what was it doing for children? The balance sheet ledger was not yet clear.

New Brunswick, New Jersey (thirty miles southwest of Times Square), was spotlighted as a kind of community case study for the impact of television on families. Dubbed "Videotown, USA," this community of 39,800 offered a close-up look at America's viewing and its priorities. More households had TVs than telephones or automobiles, and the multiset household pattern was developing. Viewing had cut deeply into the social patterns of the town. Instead of children playing stickball and parents going to the movies or joining bowling leagues, the entertainment center was now the living room. Confided one mother, "We all stay home now. TV is wonderful." And another commented, "The only thing I don't like about TV is that it takes up so much of my time."[17] But time was not the only family concern. As we could see in the Kefauver Committee's Senate Hearings of 1954, the undercurrent of concern about what television was doing to children reached well beyond "Videotown" and would be destined to surface intermittently.

By now the child-television connection was finding elaborate expression in daily humor, and much of it reflected the underlying awareness of a problem and implicit concern:

Children are no longer afraid of the dark. They just call the TV repairman.

The only time that kids look up to their parents is when they shut off the TV set.

TV sets will never replace teachers in the lower grades, anyway, until they make a model that removes snow suits and blows noses.[18]

The concern and the undercurrent persisted in a public unsure of what to make of its rectangular family member . . . even in fun.

Conclusion

It was ironic that television's most spectacular programming era took root in society's age of fear. As John Crosby said of television, "It was new and we were very innocent." The spectacular and the new have a natural way of associating with each other, and it was assuredly a time when the public wanted to be innocent. Ages of fear and suspicion take their emotional toll, and television's world of the moral absolutes held a valuable tranquilizing potential. Perhaps in the 1950s more than in any other decade, TV served as a viewer getaway to a world of innocence and simplicity. It also served as the springboard for young, future greats in the entertainment industry.

The word *classic* is frequently associated with many television programs of the fifties, and it is natural to ask why the association is so readily made and what it connotes. Age itself is not sufficient to create a classic. The term requires some combination of high quality, distinctiveness, and creative or innovative expression. Most of these elements characterized the spectacular in fifties programming. Establishing its programming identity apart from radio required that television be distinctive and innovative, and a milieu in which a "Playhouse 90" episode could provide the catalyst for daily interaction and conversation was definitely a high quality milieu. From a children's perspective, the best of the era had strong characters and role models. The initial emphasis had been more so on quality and distinctiveness than on mass marketing a program product, and the innocence and simplicity of children's programming held its own special appeal. In addition, live television had a kind of unpolished, wholesome honesty that would not get edited prior to airing. The talent was strong, the landscape was new, and programming innocence was winsome. Young television had demonstrated a power to package political candidates, a power to elevate demagogues—a power to persuade and to sell. Children as a market would experience this power more intensely as television moved from its age of innocence into the 1960s.

References

1. John Crosby, "It Was New and We Were Very Innocent," *TV Guide* (September 22, 1973), p. 5.

2. Crosby, "It Was New and We Were Very Innocent," pp. 5–8.

3. Richard B. Morris, ed., *Encyclopedia of American History* (New York: Harper and Row, 1982), pp. 519–520.

4. Jeffrey D. Merritt, *Day by Day, the Fifties* (New York: Facts on File, 1979).

5. Erik Barnouw, *The Golden Web: A History of Broadcasting in the United States*, Vol. 2 (New York: Oxford University Press, 1968), pp. 216–309.

6. Mickey Spillane, *One Lonely Night* (New York: E.P. Dutton and Company, 1951).

7. Douglas T. Miller and Marion Nowak, *The Fifties: The Way We Really Were* (Garden City, N.Y.: Doubleday and Company, 1977).

8. *New York Times* (September 24, 1950), p. 12 X; (September 30, 1951), p. 12 X; (September 28, 1952), p. 15 X; (September 27, 1953), p. 15 X.

9. E. Felix, *Television: Its Methods and Uses* (New York: McGraw-Hill, 1931).

10. Gary H. Grossman, *Saturday Morning TV* (New York: Dell, 1981).

11. *New York Times* (September 27, 1953), p. 15 X.

12. *Saturday Morning TV*, pp. 29–99.

13. Christopher Finch, *The Art of Walt Disney: From Mickey Mouse to the Magic Kingdom* (New York: H.N. Abrams, 1973).

14. "Howdy Doody Is Ten," *TV Guide* (December 28, 1957), p. 31.

15. Judiciary Committee, United States Senate, Subcommittee to Investigate Juvenile Delinquency, Part 16, *Effects on Young People of Violence and Crime Portrayed on Television* (Washington, D.C.: U.S. Government Printing Office, 1965).

16. "Looking Around," *TV Guide* (December 28, 1957).

17. "This Is Videotown, U.S.A.," *TV Guide* (April 9, 1955), pp. 4–5.

18. "The Children's Hour," *TV Guide* (December 28, 1957), p. 31.

2
A Question of Standards

As television roamed its 1960s landscape the wide eyes that had viewed the world in terms of the spectacular had now become the open eyes of bitter realities. In the 1960s, television brought us violence with an unprecedented immediacy and intensity. At the same time, television achieved profits that far exceeded radio's wildest imaginings. And therein lay the rub—keeping profitability respectable while keeping respectability profitable. Where were the bounds? What was television's true image? The questions had a poignancy befitting the decade.

A Decade Out-of-Bounds

Beginning in dreams and ending in nightmares, the 1960s felt like a decade running violently out-of-bounds with no way to call "time." A turbulent fabric with complexly interwoven violence, it was a decade described as "a time of passion, a time to burn, and a time to grieve."[1] Its triumphs seemed eclipsed by its tragedies as a youthful idealism plunged headlong into troughs of despair. From the rice paddies of Vietnam to the television mourning of a fallen president, the decade and its shocks would be indelibly etched in the lives of the American people. The 1960s was a war decade at home and abroad. The war abroad was Vietnam while the war at home was the civil rights movement. Each had its charismatic leader and an early idealism. Each had its stark encounter with death, tragedy, and loss.

The shadow of Vietnam covered the entire decade of the 1960s. U.S. involvement began modestly in 1960 with supplies and advisers to the anti-Communist forces fighting in Laos. When the Communist rebellion in South Vietnam intensified in 1962, President John F. Kennedy committed several thousand U.S. troops to support inexperienced South Vietnamese forces. Following the murder of the unpopular South Vietnamese President Diem on November 1, 1963, the United States became more deeply entangled in unsuccessful efforts to establish a stable government in South Vietnam. In 1964, President Johnson dramatically escalated U.S. involvement in response to minor naval skirmishes in the Gulf of Tonkin and a rebel attack against a U.S. base in Pleiku. The events themselves were minor, but Johnson's decision was major—to bomb North Vietnam for the first time. Early in 1965, U.S. warplanes began regular attacks against North Vietnam, and U.S. troop strength skyrocketed from 20,000 at the end of 1964 to 185,000 at the end of 1965. With the dramatic escalation came equally dramatic escalation in combat fatalities. From 1961 to 1964, 239 American lives had been lost; in 1965, there were 1,404 fatalities. Troop strength swelled to 380,000 by the end of 1966, and 474,300 by the end of 1967. With antiwar protest building in the United States, and the most devastating Communist offensive coming in January 1968, President Johnson ordered a halt to the bombing of North Vietnam. American and North Vietnamese delegations met for negotiations. Militarily, the United States had reached a standoff. Politically and in terms of lives lost, it had suffered a major defeat. The troop pullout began in 1969 as President Richard M. Nixon signaled the war's de-escalation. U.S. soldiers began returning home to a cold reception from a nation still struggling with the war it wanted to forget.

The war at home—a war for civil rights—began the 1960s peacefully with a black college student sit-in at a segregated lunch counter in Greensboro, North Carolina. Similar sit-ins followed throughout the South. "Freedom riders" focused on segregated interstate bus station facilities in 1961, and the University of Mississippi took center stage in 1962 as federal troops enforced a U.S. Supreme Court order admitting black applicant, James Meredith. The movement escalated significantly in 1963, the one hundredth anniversary of Abraham Lincoln's Emancipation Proclamation.

In April 1963, Rev. Martin Luther King, Jr., led protest marches in Birmingham, Alabama, giving the nation its first televised taste of police dog and cattle prod intimidation. King gave a moving speech in August 1963 to 200,000 demonstrators gathered at the Lincoln Memorial. They were gathered in support of President Kennedy's proposed legislation against discrimination in public facilities, school segregation, and voting restrictions. In the aftermath of Kennedy's proposed legislation and the Lincoln Memorial demonstration, resistance in the deep South heightened in 1964. Whites charged with bombing black homes frequently were not convicted, dozens of black churches were set ablaze, and the night skies of Mississippi and Alabama reflected the glow of the Ku Klux Klan's burning crosses. Several young northern whites came south to aid in voter registration drives, and three of them—James Chaney, Michael Schwerner, and Andrew Goodman—were killed in Mississippi. The war at home was making advances, but it too was experiencing tragic personal loss.

Blacks in the North rioted in 1965. Sparked by the arrest of a black by a white policeman, the Watts riot broke out in Los Angeles in August with six days of marauding, pillaging, fires, and gun battles that left forty-three dead. Black militants surfaced prominently in 1966, opposing King's nonviolent approach to equal rights. Threatening violence if their demands were not met, the militants alienated many whites. Again summer riots broke out in major northern cities such as Chicago and Cleveland. The crescendo of northern rioting reached its tragic peak in the summer of 1967 as major violence spread to more cities. July rioting in Newark claimed twenty-six lives, and the nation's worst race riot of the century spanned five days in Detroit, requiring Army troop intervention and leaving forty-three dead. King's assassination, in April 1968, touched off a wave of violence in cities across the nation. It was a tide that would require 55,000 troops for containment and would leave forty-nine dead. The tide gradually abated in 1969 with less urban disorder, and continued gains for blacks in elective offices and in housing opportunities. Focus now turned from the war-torn streets to the courthouses as job discrimination became the new focus. The war at home had taken its toll, but its gains had been far more visible than those in Vietnam.

Assassinations further darkened the nation's violent sixties. This generation had never experienced the assassination of a president, and the nation of many became a nation united in shock and grief. Anyone old enough to remember could tell you where they were on November 22, 1963, when they received the tragic news that John F. Kennedy had been assassinated. There would be other dates to remember such as April 4, 1968, when Rev. Martin Luther King, Jr. was assassinated, and June 5, 1968, when Robert F. Kennedy fell victim to an assassin's bullets. Violence seemed endemic to the times as it continued to shock and numb its people.[2, 3]

The youth movement of the 1960s was deeply affected by each aspect of the decade's turbulence. The generation consisted of postwar baby boomers, reared in the permissiveness of Dr. Benjamin Spock, and rocked in the cradle of television. Coming from the affluent American middle class, the generation was characterized as being full of ecstatic and nonrational consumers of forty-second news stories rather than sober, linear readers of newspapers. Television had brought the charisma of a young president, and the generation's idealism embraced his dream. That idealism and the nightmare of Kennedy's death would affect young people very deeply, and in turn these people would find many avenues to express their despair and disillusionment.

The threads of the youth movement were as complex as the decade itself. There were hippies, yippies, new leftists, flower children, and others—a loose-knit confederation of television-conscious young people who rallied and demonstrated in response to vocal anti-establishment leaders, causes, and lifestyles. The Vietnam War was an early rallying point, and although the protesters were but a small fraction of the student population on campuses across the country, they were a leading edge of dissent, which would grow among their peers, intellectuals, and the population at large as the decade wore on. When the Kent State University tragedy of May 1970 vividly focused the image of armed National Guardsmen killing unarmed college students, a wave of student protest gripped and closed several universities, and there was little tolerance left for violence either at home or abroad. By mid-1970, nine out of ten young people and a majority of the general public were antiwar.[4] The youth movement had offended its elders and the general public, but it also had affected their attitudes on a basic issue.

Television Programming in the Out-of-Bounds

It was inevitable that the 1960s would be an era of standards in programming. Television had wandered far from its spectacular 1950s landscape, and there was question of how far was too far. Television's golden age of programming was now being tempered by assassinations, war, violence, and money. Each had an impact, and each carried ripples that would reach its young.

The money ripple came early, and reverberations from it reached well beyond the decade. President Kennedy had appointed an unknown, Newton Minow, to chair the Federal Communications Commission (FCC). When mild-mannered Minow opened his address to the 1961 convention of the National Association of Broadcasters (NAB), he appeared to know his place and to be staying in it. He spoke of NAB's courage, acknowledged the difficulties in its work, and cited its financial health. He praised NAB's 1960 gross revenues of $1,268,000,000, and noted that the $243.9 million profits meant a 19.2 percent return on investment. Then as broadcasting executives began to ease back and relax in their after-dinner seats, the current of Minow's comments shifted:

> I invite you to sit down in front of your television set when your station goes on the air and stay there without a book, magazine, newspaper, profit and loss sheet or rating book to distract you—and keep your eyes glued to that set until the station signs off. I can assure you that you will observe a vast wasteland.[5] (p. 197)

Those last two words hung in the air like an ominous cloud. They were words that might stay in remission for a time, but would break out all too regularly for an industry's liking.

The first outbreak came in a spy-glass look at the 1961 season.[6] "The best season in at least five years!" (p. 19) said TV critic Harriet Van Horne as she recounted the star-studded hits. What's more, it had been a season of frontier-space lift-off as John Glenn made his historic journey. But the year also had much that left viewers angry and confused. In the words of writer Roger Youman: "The moments of glory . . . may not outlive the memory of one supremely tasteless hour of television. When the history of TV is written years from now, this one hour may stigmatize 1961–62 as a season of ignominy"

(p. 21). He was referring to ABC's December 3 episode of "Bus Stop" (episode named "A Lion Walks Among Us"), that "parlayed sex, violence and the animal magnetism of its star (a teenager's dreamboat called Fabian) into an hour of unalloyed sensationalism, cynically calculated to attract the youthful viewers" (pp. 21–22). Critics considered it an indefensible violation of the network's own TV code and a flagrant breach of good taste. ABC admitted it had made a mistake. Said Youman, "The 'Bus Stop' affair was a symptom of an infectious TV disease—the brutal competition for high ratings at any price" (p. 22).

There was hope that "Bus Stop" would bring sober reflection on network television's responsibility to its nation's youth, but no one seriously believed a tasteless "Bus Stop" episode would curtail ratings competition. With the purpose of television being sales rather than a disinterested artistic depiction of life, writer Alistair Cooke felt it important that TV critics not take too seriously either themselves or public pressure.[7] He saw television as the most lucrative branch of merchandising ever created in the United States, "the simple truth we have to recognize at the beginning" (p. 9). Acknowledging that Newton Minow's wasteland had served as a catalyst for new programs "that genuinely perform the public service of alerting the Nation to the present state of its mental health "(p. 9), he was ultimately aware that "the primary aim of the television business is to persuade more people to buy more goods, some of them dubious in value, some of the spiels unethical in content" (p. 10). Hence, ratings competition! As new ratings battles laced the 1962 season headlines, one had the impression that even a tasteless "Bus Stop" episode or its counterpart would be included if the ratings warranted.

"Wasteland" Sensitivity

The industry's sensitivity after Minow's speech surfaced in both its dominant formats and its prosocial programming for children. Comedy had been the most resilient and successful format throughout television's history, but it had characteristics that made it especially appealing to networks in the aftermath of Minow's "wasteland" and ABC's "Bus Stop." Socially naive comedy was safe. Not only had it been the single most dominant format in ratings successes, but it was noncontroversial. Comedy rarely dealt with racial, religious, or economic conflicts that could potentially offend parts of the audience, and it did not emotionally involve viewers to the point where they might either ignore or become irritated by commercials. These factors, in combination with comedy's greatest statistical likelihood of getting top ratings, made it a natural for an era when television wanted a safe yet successful profile. Although standards concerns and the reverberations of Minow's speech dominated this television era, there were some notable, positive features in children's programming. Some of the notables were undoubtedly reactive programming, while other programs would have been successful in any case. Among the latter, "National Velvet" aired in the fall of 1960. As a Lassie-with-hoofs, it carried much the same appeal as America's favorite dog. For example, one program gave young viewers the homespun message that "Sometimes the truth's worth a heap more 'n' the winnin'." That same year Shirley Temple hosted a Sunday evening series on NBC that brought a range of classics including "Winnie the Pooh," "The Village Blacksmith," "Little Men," and the "Ray Bradbury Science Fiction Chiller for Kids."[8] "Walt Disney" was in the process of switching to NBC and becoming one of the few shows to be produced in color. NBC and its peacock logo would usher in the color era.

Added programming for children came in the 1962 season. NBC added "Marx Magic Midway," a circus show, to its late Saturday morning schedule, and followed it with "Exploring," an educational series for children in the five- to eleven-year-old age group, covering music, mathematics, social studies, science, and language. CBS counterprogrammed "Exploring" with "Reading Room." Designed for eight- to twelve-year-olds, it featured an educator-selected book-of-the-week discussed by a panel of children. ABC added "Discovery '62," a weekday late-afternoon show designed to educate and entertain, bringing children such events as the hatching of a baby chick, and a day with a Parisian schoolboy. And ABC was inviting children of all ages to tune in on late Sunday afternoons for "Wild Kingdom," built from the background of ABC's earlier "Zoo Parade" and featuring the "Zoo Parade" host, Marlin Perkins (director of Chicago's Lincoln Park Zoo).[9]

Other postwasteland programming most visibly took the form of specials. A spin-off from the spectaculars of the 1950s specials had the advantages of garnering ratings without the expensive, long-term commitment of a weekly series. In both the general and the children's programming context, specials were quite prevalent in the 1963 season. The lineup seemed reminiscent of the 1950s golden age in programming. The heavyweights included "The Bell Telephone Hour," "Young People's Concerts," the "NBC Opera Company," the "Royal Ballet," the "DuPont Show of the Week," "Hallmark Hall of Fame," and "Hedda Gabler." The specials syndrome was fueled by high ratings, and peaked in 1967. In their review of the 1967 season, *TV Guide* editors called it either "the beginning of television's second Golden Age or the end of serious efforts to upgrade the medium with special programming."[10] The fate of TV programming depended heavily on networks, advertisers, and the viewers. If networks would refrain from counterprogramming specials, they could extend the quality of program hours available to viewers. Whether advertisers invested in these expensive undertakings also was a critical factor. And, of course, viewers needed to do their part by tuning in.

The season proved to be a specials success and the trend continued. CBS and NBC punctuated Saturday morning cartoons with one-hour specials. There was "Children's Hour" from CBS, based on the adventures of child-heroes from diverse social backgrounds, and "American Rainbow" from ABC presented a range of one-hour programs extending from "Hot Dog" (a frank look at familiar items of Americana) to "Wilderness Road" (a fatherless boy heading West).

"Winnie the Pooh and the Honey Tree," a 1965 movie short, was being brought to television, and a new Peanuts special, "It Was a Short Summer, Charlie Brown," joined the popular ranks of its forerunners. "Horton Hears a Who," "Goldilocks," and "Frosty the Snowman" premiered, and "Babar Comes to America" joined the popular previous season sequel "Babar the Elephant." Perhaps the most significant network special was NBC's "Hey, Hey, Hey—It's Fat Albert." Described as "turning Bill Cosby's frisky boyhood buddies into cartoon characters",[11] it was destined to turn a significant children's programming corner as well. Cosby was in a unique position to identify with black children, their setting, and their needs, and the program would heighten awareness among all its child viewers.

The most significant children's programming of the 1967 season came from outside the commercial networks. After two years lead time and $8 million, Children's Television Workshop was launching "Sesame Street." This innovative, exhaustively researched series for preschoolers began its live one-hour programs on November 10. Impressed by the effectiveness of advertising techniques in holding children's attention, founder Joan Ganz Cooney conceptualized the integration of these techniques—hard sell, jingles, cute cartoons, live action—to teach the three Rs and basic reasoning skills. Trying to reach the ghetto, inner-city preschooler, the program's primary goal was to prepare children for reading by the time they entered school. It was a landmark experiment set up jointly by the Carnegie Corporation, the Ford Foundation, and the U.S. Office of Education. In addition to "Sesame Street," the season included sixty-five new color episodes of "Mister Rogers' Neighborhood" and forty additional programs of "What's New."[12]

The 1960s brought notable program classics for young viewers. By 1969, ABC's "Discovery" was in its eighth year. It had been able to rate as well as Saturday morning television shows. NBC's "Children's Theater" had produced twelve live-action dramas since its early 1960s inception. Among them were "Stuart Little," "The Reluctant Dragon," "Little Women," "The Enormous Egg" and "Robin Hood." And the newly inaugurated series of specials from CBS "Children's Hour" promised to bring similar themes and quality. One of its specials, "JT," was destined to become a classic. Some of the finest in children's programming had come in this era with high quality especially strong in 1969.

Programs in Transition

The realities of the marketplace beyond the "Bus Stop" had greeted children on the doorstep of the 1960s. Their long-time friend, "Howdy Doody," was leaving. The announcement of Howdy's departure came quietly. In the schedule of Saturday, September 24, 1960, the 10 A.M. slot read simply:

> In this special one-hour show, everybody in Doodyville is packing up and getting ready to leave town. And Clarabell has a secret.

The caption beneath it had an equally simple message:

> Last show of the series. Next week Shari Lewis and her puppets begin a half-hour program on Channel 5.[13]

More than a decade in Doodyville had come to its quiet end.

Captain Kangaroo had become to children what his mentor Bob Smith had been to their parents. He was equated with the wholesome and with standing up for children's ideals even when the advertising revenue years had been lean. He refused to take the step that would buckle on principle and advertise products that would be potentially hazardous to young viewers. Vitamins and the concept of pill taking was an example of this sensitivity. The Captain, Keeshan, knew young children's potential for accidentally taking dad or mom's sleeping pills, and he rejected any ads that had the possibility of disastrous outcomes. He also rejected food jokes ("Food is a precious commodity"), the exhibition of frightened or badly trained animals ("A wild bird beating its wings frantically against the cage is a cruel sight"), and magicians who disappeared or locked themselves into trunks and closets ("We don't do things that might lead a child to try them and get asphyxiated"). Parents felt they had a friend in "Captain Kangaroo," the only six-day-a-week program for children on network television. The depth of parent devotion is summarized in a letter Keeshan received from a Haverford, Pennsylvania, woman: "My son is three years old, Captain, and believe it or not, before he was born I used to dream of the day when I would have a child to watch your engaging show."[14] Although "Captain Kangaroo" and "Shari Lewis" were still airborne, the ranks of live TV, hosts, and puppetry were notably dwindling. Children were discovering cartoons. The organization of citizen action groups would not be far behind.

The 1960s would bring an animation avalanche. Movie cartoon celebrities like Bugs Bunny were coming to television. Bugs made his grand entrance in the fall of 1960, joined by Sylvester and Tweety, and skunk charmer Pepe Le Pew. His Saturday morning debut came in 1962 and stretched to one-hour when Roadrunner joined him in 1968. These were cartoon characters who had made their fame among adult movie audiences.

Hanna-Barbera's creative instincts and partial animation techniques pioneered a new breed of children's friends. "Yogi Bear from Jellystone Park" was a lovable all-time favorite that put the Hanna-Barbera Studio very much in the limelight. Other creations from its studio included "Ruff and Reddy" (the first cartoon characters it had done for TV, 1957), "Huckleberry Hound" (1958 inspiration for spin-off "Yogi"), "The Flintstones" (among the longest running series in prime time and Saturday morning, premiering Saturdays in

1967), "The Jetsons" (twenty-first-century family coming to Saturday mornings in 1963), "Top Cat" (celebrated talking cat, Saturday debut in 1963), "Tom and Jerry" (1940s movie veterans returning in 1965), "Scooby-Doo" (premiering in 1969 but destined for 1970s Saturday stardom), and a host of others. Other studios in the 1960s could not match the Hanna-Barbera presence in size or popularity, but some of these studios had well-known characters—folks like Mighty Mouse and Heckle and Jeckle from Terrytoons—were riding 1950s fame into this era, whereas Walter Lantz's Woody Woodpecker rode in with celebrity status built all the way from the early 1940s.[15]

Detectives, Westerns, and space heroes frequently found their way into Saturday morning animation. John Glenn's historic 1961 journey in space provided the catalyst for several Saturday morning space programs, and the fascination with that frontier continued to be a recurring theme. Cross-overs from prime time to Saturday morning happened, but were relatively infrequent. Adult prime-time shows were not made available for Saturday morning animation at their ratings peak because the networks did not want anything to happen to their property that might adversely affect ratings. Cross-overs were more likely to occur when a program had tailed off in the prime time-ratings, and the frequency of cross-overs would be much more pronounced in the 1970s.

Perhaps a more significant impact on Saturday mornings in the 1960s was the specials concept. Its one-hour length was generating cartoon-superhero shows that were stretching beyond their thirty-minute bounds, and this trend was destined to continue. The success of movies in prime time also had its Saturday morning impact. For example, the 1969 season brought a two-hour drama entitled "The Shepherd of the Hills," featuring a high-spirited mountain girl in love with a reckless young man. This kind of two-hour venture was unprecedented for Saturday morning. Another adult format, the game show, was successful for a short time on Saturday mornings. ABC had added "Shenanigans" to its 1964 Saturday lineup, but the concept proved short-lived. The specials format, animated program clones from adult prime-time hits, and the general prevalence of the comedy theme in adult as well as children's programming, were far more pervasive Saturday morning influences.[16] The day clearly belonged to cartoons.

Growing Concerns About Standards

Cartoons would neither outrun nor escape the mood of growing public concern. Perhaps the wasteland cloud in their very first year had set the tone. And the tasteless "Bus Stop" episode had aroused concerns relating to program content and broadcast standards. Whatever the network standards, there was insufficient protection for young viewers, and concern was building. Standards practices at the three networks were coming into question, and the spotlight revealed a case-by-case network treatment of potentially problematic incidents.

On questions of acceptability and good taste, opinions differed among standards executives and even within the networks themselves. There were inconsistencies between editors, networks, and even the New York and Hollywood offices of the same network. Where Hollywood might have more tendency to remember the Bible Belt, New York might seem more sophisticated. Writer Leslie Raddatz considered NBC the most sensitive of the three networks in the area of mental health, frowning on words such as "crazy" and "nuts," even when they were not being used to refer to mental illness. Bob Wood at NBC considered ABC the tightest on "damns" and "hells," and ABC's Dorothy Brown— who had okayed the Fabian "Bus Stop" show—agreed that she had a ban on both words. Meanwhile, CBS's word-count veteran, W.H. Tankersley, observed that the last season's Hollywood-originated network programs used only two "damns" and no "hells". Standards executives were caught between sensitive producers on the one hand, and public acceptance on the other, while functioning with a set of rules that changed from day to day and hour to hour. Continuity acceptance editors appeared to be a hard-working group who were conscientious about their work, but dared not take themselves too seriously.

Continuity acceptance was a term that had been adopted to bypass the connotations of censorship. Producers would admit that continuity acceptance fulfilled a useful function. In the words of producer Leslie Stevens, "Producers are the gas that makes the car run. Continuity acceptance is the brake that keeps it from going over the cliff."[17] And writer Leslie Raddatz notes, "Of course, there was one occasion when the brake didn't quite make the bus stop."[18]

The children's equivalent of Bus Stop dawned with New Year's Day 1965. Soupy Sales, a child idol from the fifties, suggested that his WNEW early morning child viewers go to the wallets of their sleeping fathers, take out "some of those funny green pieces of paper with all those nice pictures of George Washington, Abraham Lincoln, and Alexander Hamilton, and send them along to your old pal, Soupy, care of WNEW, New York." Advertisers Helitzer and Heyel reported that enough money poured in to constitute "the biggest heist since the Boston Brink's robbery." The tremendous vulnerability of young viewers surfaced. Knowing to what extent young viewers followed their idols left an all the more unsettling feeling about the messages that adolescent viewers would find in "Bus Stop." The Soupy Sales incident would continue to surface in the years and even decades ahead.[19]

Dr. Benjamin Spock, author of the veritable bible for young mothers, found that he could no longer take lightly the child's viewing experience of violence and killing. He feared that we were glorifying violence and perpetuating our unjust treatment of Indians, blacks, and waves of immigrants. He was pained by the TV coverage of bombing and burning of Vietnamese men, women, and children since much of it was accessible to child viewing. Spock's awareness of the horrors of war and nuclear weapons made him believe that we need to "build into our children a horror of violence, a devotion to civilized ways of settling disputes, a real consideration for the feelings of other people." He felt television let viewers down in these respects. An example was a network decision to preempt the Senate Foreign Relations Committee's first hearings on the Vietnam issue in favor of airing cartoon reruns. Spock was not without hope, but he feared what he perceived as television's laboratory for violence instruction and its tendencies to entertain rather than educate.[20]

Others shared Spock's concern; among them was Professor Louis Kronenberger of Brandeis University. Kronenberger called commercial television "uncivilized and uncivilizing." Acknowledging its finer moments and triumphs, his concern centered on the content and underlying values of commercial programming—sex, violence, gossip, material success, and cash. In his view, "there has been nothing too elegant for it to coarsen, too sacred for it to profane."[21] And there was further concern that television was engaged in world pollution for profit. Critic Samuel Grafton said, "We're flooding the world's TV screens with the worst of American TV—and very little of the best." There was the feeling that we were exporting a two-class image of American people, "the wild ones who shoot each other and the rich ones who drive big cars and don't have to work."[22]

TV Guide reflected the extensiveness of this concern as it published an unprecedented eight-part series entitled "What Is TV Doing to Them?" Focusing concerns within network television programming, the series examined several facets of the child-viewing picture. National Educational Television (NET) Director Paul Taft expressed concerns about the interpersonal relationships depicted on television: "They hit each other, they solve their problems with force. This leads to a breakdown of youngsters' feelings about how friends should be treated."[23] Taft's comments verbalized many of the concerns that already were mobilizing citizen and governmental initiatives.

Saturday morning's animation scene generated its own special discomfort when researchers such as Alberta Siegel pointed out that cartoons ranked among the most violent programming on television.[24]

Citizen Action

In January 1968, a handful of mothers in Newton, Massachusetts, shared their concerns about the content of programming their children were watching. Initial concern centered on television violence, but they quickly concluded that it was just one element in an overall picture of poor program quality. They also knew violence would be very hard to define and that a singular focus on it would quickly transport them into the muddy turf of developing censorship guidelines. Almost a year of meetings and heated discussions led the mothers to the conclusion that they did not want their children to be vulnerable to television marketing, and this issue would be their focal mission. In 1968, then, they formally organized as Action for Children's Television (ACT). Evelyn Kaye became the group's first president, and members began to monitor television and programming. At first their monitoring was local, and their concerns quickly collided with the program "Romper Room." A show born in the early 1950s, "Romper Room" epitomized the host-selling approach with a diverse array of its own merchandise. ACT took issue with this approach and carried their concern well into the 1970s. Much would be heard from action groups on the national level in the decade ahead.[25]

Another citizen action organization was taking root during the White House conference on Food, Nutrition, and Health meeting in December 1969. Robert Choate would head this group, known as the Council on Children, Media and Merchandising (CCMM), and their mission would become nutrition content in food advertised to children, specifically breakfast cereals.[26]

Governmental Initiatives

With the turbulent 1960s came a violence-ridden milieu that was ripe for governmental study initiatives. Following up on the work of the 1954 Subcommittee on Juvenile Delinquency, that same subcommittee surveyed television program content in 1961 and 1964, and concluded that violence depicted on television was greater in frequency than it had been a decade earlier. Senator Thomas Dodd, chairing the subcommittee, was especially concerned that the most violent programs of the 1961–1962 season were now syndicated and being widely distributed and shown on independent networks and stations. The subcommittee reiterated psychiatrist Frederic Wertham's charge that television had become a school for violence. Using their barometer of the ratings and the marketplace, the networks continued programming as usual.

With the continuing impact of violence, rioting, and demonstrations came a strong initiative by President Lyndon B. Johnson. He appointed the National Commission on the Causes and Prevention of Violence and gave it the mandate to conduct a penetrating examination of American life, past and present—traditions, institutions, culture, customs, laws—to understand and remedy the social forces producing violence. The commission was chaired by Dr. Milton Eisenhower, and in an early stage of its work it created a task force on the media. Established in June 1968, the Eisenhower Commission was given a year to complete its report. Under a deadline extension from President Richard M. Nixon, the commission's final report was submitted in December 1969.

With its limited lifetime, the Eisenhower Commission focused on opinions and recommendations of the top authorities in communications, academia, and governmental agencies. An attempt was made to synthesize and report existing television research, but the studies were relatively sparse and scattered, and many of them utilized film rather than television programming. The commission acknowledged the danger and the potential for television scapegoating, and made a very strong statement on televised violence. The report concluded that a constant diet of viewing TV violence adversely affected attitudes and character. Specific reference was made to a television emphasis on violent, antisocial behavior and violence in social life being fostered on television as a moral and social value. The report placed the burden of remedy on commercial television itself, and warned that if such changes were not forthcoming, the public had changing power that reached well beyond governmental commissions. The power being cited was that of citizen action groups such as ACT.

As the work of the Eisenhower Commission got underway, concern was growing in Congress as well. Thoughts from the original Kefauver Subcommittee Report lingered uncomfortably in the minds of current congressmen, and one of the most concerned was Senator John Pastore, chairman of the Senate Subcommittee on Communications. His television-related concern had a long history. He became subcommittee chairman in 1955, and began looking closely at the television industry during the quiz show scandals of 1958–1959. As early as 1962, he expressed his sex/violence programming concerns before the National Association of Broadcasters, but at the same time he was wary of trespassing on First Amendment freedoms. This meant he preferred to bring network executives into public, exerting informal pressure and fostering self-regulation. Pastore's concern deepened as assassinations and riots became widespread, but he hesitated to duplicate investigative effort. Knowing that the Joint Committee for Research on Television and Children had been established through the Senate Judiciary Committee in 1963, and well aware of the Eisenhower Commission's work, he waited. No report was forthcoming from the judiciary committee study, and early 1968 rumors suggested that the Eisenhower Commission Report would not only be late, but it would not address the issue of televised violence. Pastore felt he had waited long enough. On March 5, 1968, he wrote to the Health, Education, and Welfare (HEW) secretary, Robert Finch, asking him to request that the Surgeon General appoint a committee to study and scientifically establish, to whatever extent possible, the existence and nature of the effects of television-violence programming on children. Pastore gave the Surgeon General wide discretionary powers in committee member selection, but it was clear that he wanted social scientists to be prominently represented.

Secretary Finch acted quickly in response to Senator Pastore's letter. Within one week, Dr. William H. Stewart, Surgeon General, talked with Pastore and members of the subcommittee. He then appeared before the subcommittee in open hearings to agree with Pastore's initiative and the nation's need to be informed. President Nixon's personal endorsement of the initiative was received in March, and formal authorization for the Surgeon General's Advisory Committee on Television and Social Behavior came from Secretary Finch in mid-April.

There were complex procedural and funding questions to be addressed, and the general question of advisory committee membership would prove a challenging one. Soliciting nominations from professional organizations including the American Psychological Association, the American Sociological Association, and the American Psychiatric Association, nominations also were requested from the National Association of Broadcasters (NAB), ABC, CBS, and NBC. From a compilation of 200 names, a final list of 40 were sent to the network presidents and the chief executive of NAB for review. While CBS affirmed the list as distinguished and made no selection suggestions, responses from ABC, NBC, and the NAB raised objections to 7 names. Consequently, two distinguished psychologists whose research related directly to this field— Albert Bandura and Leonard Berkowitz—were not among the chosen. In fact, only one of the researchers suggested by the professional and academic organizations attained committee membership. Despite a heavy industry bias, the twelve-member committee included several Ph.D. level researchers.

In his committee guidelines, Secretary Finch made it clear that the committee would confine itself to scientific findings and would not make policy recommendations. In early meetings of the committee, several significant decisions were made or implicitly agreed. The committee requested a compilation of existing research with continuous updates of new research. Decision was made to support both short-range and long-range research studies in the field, providing opportunity to examine both immediate and cumulative effects. The approach also was one of supporting diverse types of proposals and research initiatives rather than supporting one large-scale study or giving constant liaison input. Part of the rationale for this open-ended approach was to encourage proposal submissions from young researchers in the field.

This approach was not without its critics from within and outside the committee. Some of the researchers (for example, Jack Lyle) felt the end result would be dozens of splintered pieces that were impossible to pull together meaningfully. With some misgivings the approach moved forward, and a budget of $1 million was appropriated in support of twenty-one major research studies. As we will see in chapter 3, it was destined to become the most significant and important research initiative in the TV programming field. Whether it would serve as the impetus for industry change was yet another matter. As we saw throughout the 1960s, commercial television was to be, in the final analysis, commercial.[27]

Conclusion

The Vietnam War, assassinations, public grieving, student protests, and urban riots had visual appeal, and there was little dearth of action shots and gripping visual images in the 1960s. Some of those images had an impact on viewers as profound as the events themselves. The murder of President Kennedy's assassin (Lee Harvey Oswald) covered live on nationwide television, the Kennedy children at their father's graveside, Sheriff "Bull" Conners' cattle prods and German shepherds attacking defenseless black marchers in Birmingham, a napalm-burning Vietnamese child running desperately down the road—these images and many more brought starkly to the personal level the horrors of violence and war. Television was becoming less and less an escape route into fantasy, as fantasy kept getting soaked with a vivid, indelible reality.

Television had come a long way from its beginnings when there were concerns that it not intrude on a viewer's day. Now this dominant leisure activity was on the way to breaking the six-hour-a-day viewing mark. With the advent of color and portable sets, there seemed little doubt that this trend would continue. No matter how problematic the programming, a nation wondered, worried . . . and watched.

Two generations of children held significance in the events of the 1960s—the first generation of television-raised children and those now viewing it. The first group of children to be nursed and rocked in the cradle of television had now attained adolescence, and their expression of that adolescence was no small concern to the public. Had they taken their cue from the medium that had nursed them? Would their youth movement have surfaced in any case, or was it a product of the times? Given what we know about the cumulative viewing effects of television, the role of TV nurturing likely had been a significant one. That many of television's first generation of children had turned to violence and open rebellion left an unsettled feeling about television's current children. One had to remember, however, that television's first generation had also turned to the Peace Corps and the nation's poor.

To a shocked and rattled nation that did not want to repeat the violent 1960s, television's current children were a vital concern. What were they learning from television? How would that learning affect their future and their nation's? In the midst of a violent era, these questions took on a special relevance. The years immediately ahead would bring some unsettling, although not surprising answers, as a nation of concerned citizens moved from the streets to the more orderly halls of research and the legal process.

References

1. Charles R. Morris, *A Time of Passion* (New York: Harper and Row, 1984), pp. 70–128.

2. Thomas Parker and Douglas Nelson, *Day-by-Day: The Sixties* (New York: Facts on File, Inc., 1983), pp. ix–xvi.

3. William Benton, publisher, *The Annals of America* (Chicago: Encyclopedia Brittanica, Inc., 1968), Vol. 18.

4. Tom Schachtman, *Decade of Shocks: Dallas to Watergate, 1963–1974* (New York: Poseidon Press, 1983), pp. 45–100.

5. Erik A. Barnouw, *The Image Empire: A History of Broadcasting in the United States*, Vol. 3 (New York: Oxford University Press, 1970), pp. 196–207.

6. R.J. Youman, "What Kind of Season Has It Been?" *TV Guide* (June 30, 1962), pp. 18–20.

7. Alistair Cooke, "Attention TV Critics: You Are Wasting Your Time," *TV Guide* (September 24, 1962), pp. 8–10.

8. *TV Guide* (October 1, 1960), p. A-15.

9. "Daytime TV: This Year It's Children First." *TV Guide* (September 15, 1962), p. 26.

10. "As We See the New Season," *TV Guide* (September 9, 1967), p. 1.

11. "Specials: For Children," *TV Guide* (September 13, 1969), p. 14.

12. "Educational TV," *TV Guide* (September 13, 1969), pp. 67-70.

13. *TV Guide* (September 24, 1960), p. A-3.

14. "The K Stands for Keeshan, Too," *TV Guide* (July 29, 1961), p. 4; (August 5, 1961), p. 17.

15. Gary H. Grossman, *Saturday Morning TV* (New York: Dell, 1981), pp. 6–13, 29–39.

16. *TV Guide* (October 12, 1968), pp. A-12–A-13.

17. Leslie Raddatz, "Have You Been Shocked, Outraged, or Scandalized by Television?," *TV Guide* (November 9, 1963), p. 19.

18. Raddatz, "Have You Been Shocked," p. 19.

19. Melvin Helitzer and Carl Heyel, *The Youth Market: Its Dimensions, Influence, and Opportunities for You* (New York: Media Books, 1970).

20. Benjamin Spock, "Dr. Spock Prescribes for Television," *TV Guide* (June 4, 1966), pp. 8–11.

21. Louis Kronenberger, "Uncivilized and Uncivilizing," *TV Guide* (February 25, 1966), pp. 15–19.

22. Samuel Grafton, "For Export: The Vast Wasteland," *TV Guide* (September 21, 1963), pp. 4–7.

23. Neil Hickey, "The Key Word Is Entertainment," *TV Guide* (October 18, 1969), p. 10.

24. George Gerbner, "Violence in Television Drama: Trends and Symbolic Functions," in George A. Comstock and Eli A. Rubinstein, eds., *Television and Social Behavior: Media Content and Control* (Washington, D.C.: U.S. Government Printing Office, 1972), pp. 28–187.

25. Joan Barthel, "Boston Mothers Against Kidvid," *New York Times Magazine* (January 5, 1975), pp. 14–15 ff.

26. Robert B. Choate, Presentation to the National Association of Broadcasters' Television Code Review Board, May 26, 1971.

27. Douglass Cater and Stephen Strickland, *TV Violence and the Child* (New York: Russell Sage Foundation, 1975), pp. 1–66.

3
Spotlight on Children

To look at the 1970s is to look at the history of television itself. Virtually every issue, every nuance, every struggle is here with microcosmic clarity and force. It was an era when both violence and advertising reached pinnacle investigative attention. It was an era when public television struggled for recognition amid its older commercial siblings—caught in its own family squabbles yet experiencing patches of brilliant program creativity. It was an era when social issues came more starkly to television's living room window than ever before. And it was an era when the misfortunes of ill-timed and seemingly unrelated events worked to the detriment of children—a prime-time access rule, a syndication company suit, family viewing time, and heightened public criticism of networks during their most conscientious time of self-examination. It was doubtful that there ever would be another single decade in television's history with the profound issue depth and range, as well as struggle.

Grassroots Eruption

As mothers had met in living rooms and researchers had met at the White House Conference on Food, Nutrition, and Health, they laid the groundwork for grassroots concerns that would bring children and television to center stage. Action for Children's Television (ACT), the Boston-area organization, swiftly brought its issues to the public conscience. After first taking issue with the host-selling practices of "Romper Room," the group soon turned to the national arena. ACT requested meetings with officials at each of the three networks to discuss the need for a code of ethics. Only CBS agreed to meet, and it was reluctant to institute change strictly on its own. ACT then turned to the federal government.

ACT's basic approach was to petition, and one of its first petitions was submitted to the Federal Communications Commission (FCC) in February 1970. It asked the FCC to adopt rules barring sponsorship and commercials on children's programs; barring performers from using or mentioning services, products, or stores during children's programs; and asking that each station have a minimum public service requirement of fourteen hours per week in daily programming for children.[1] The ACT initiative gained considerable public attention, and ACT leaders skillfully seized the opportunity to awaken the national conscience about the issues and about their organization. They held their first annual Symposium on Children and Television in October 1970, and this annual event became a meeting ground in which government leaders, consumer advocates, lawyers, and psychologists could discuss the issues, share their common concerns, and air their differences.

ACT's early petition effort at the FCC found a receptive hearing, and Chairman Dean Burch's 1971 speech to the American Advertising Federation made it bluntly clear that he believed children must be considered a special and notably vulnerable audience in terms of advertising. In his hand-delivered warning to top television executives, Burch said millions of viewers were "fed [up] to the teeth . . . and not about to settle for more cosmetics." He further indicated that whether commercial television was capable of providing quality children's programming would be resolved "one way or another . . . and soon." The focus was Saturday morning cartoons and commercials, and Burch indicated that while the complete removal of commmercials from children's prime time was not being threatened, those programs might be removed from Nielsen ratings competition—a move that would have a clear impact on network advertising revenues. Speaking directly to the advertising issue and a young, trusting audience, he said he found it "intolerable to seek to bilk the innocent with shoddy advertising appeals." It was, he said, "akin to statutory rape."[2]

The aftermath of the petition and Burch's speech brought mountains of mail to the FCC in support of the ACT proposal. In September 1971, Burch announced the creation of a permanent children's unit within the FCC. Meanwhile, ACT petitioned the Federal Trade Commission (FTC) to prohibit all televised toy advertising, food product advertising, and vitamin advertising directed toward children.

ACT's early initiatives soon gained victories. In 1972—just three months after the petition against vitamin advertising to children—the three drug companies named in the petition voluntarily withdrew their child-directed ads. Another victory came in January 1973, when the National Association of Broadcasters (NAB) wrote a change into their television code, prohibiting host selling in children's programs and reducing the allowable advertising time per hour from 16 minutes to 12. The following year the NAB announced further reductions in that limit during children's weekend programming—down to 10 minutes per hour by 1974, and 9½ minutes per hour by 1975. ABC was announcing that it would make even further reductions—down to 7½ minutes by 1980.[3] Carefully focused grassroots efforts were having an impact in Washington.

By the mid-1970s, a mixed picture characterized the ACT accomplishments. Its victories had been significant ones that would make a lasting difference, but the basic moving force of the TV industry toward profits would bring defeat to ACT's key goals. One such defeat came from the FCC when it issued its 1974 report on the children's programming issue. While acknowledging broadcasters' special responsibility to children and the possible need for special safeguards, it did not adopt any of ACT's petition elements. In the FCC perspective, children's programming and advertising practices would be left to industry self-regulation. Burch's address to top-level executives in 1971 had sounded convincing, but the product of the commission was far less so.

By the second half of the 1970s, one could expect ACT petitions to receive more attention, and it was the FTC that heard ACT's petition of the mid and late 1970s. On April 16, 1977, the FTC received an ACT petition requesting a ban on candy advertising addressed to children. Ten days later, the FTC received a petition from Center for Science in the Public Interest (CSPI), seeking a ban on child-directed television advertising for snacks deriving more than ten percent of their calories from added sugar. CSPI also was seeking mandatory affirmative disclosure of the added sugar content in advertised foods as well as the dental health risks.

The two petitions had a broad and impressive support base. Representatives of eleven national organizations met with FTC Chairman Pertschuk to endorse the petitions. These organizations represented a wide cross-section of child-related interests, and included such entities as the American Academy of Pediatrics, the American Public Health Association, the Black Child Welfare League of America, the National Association of Elementary School Principals, and the National Women's Political Caucus. The initiative also had the support of key officials in the Food and Drug Administration, and the Department of Health, Education, and Welfare. Few efforts have ever received support of that magnitude and diversity.

The FTC's Staff Report on TV Advertising to Children was released to the public on February 27, 1978. Its proposed rule making urged a ban on all advertising directed to children too young to understand selling intent, and a ban on sugar food ads seen by significant numbers of eight- to eleven-year-olds (foods considered significant dental health risks). For less hazardous sugared food ads to this age group the advertisers were asked to fund balancing nutritional/health disclosures. The report and the testimony relating to it had been a milestone in federal agency focus on a child-based television issue. Its incorporation of testimony and research had been equally impressive and exemplary. Like the decade itself, the report was unique.[4]

From the White House Conference on Food, Nutrition, and Health came 500 reform recommendations for President Nixon. The conference also spawned the Council on Children, Media and Merchandising, which targeted cereals advertised to children. "Empty calories" soon came into middle-class vocabularies, and with that awareness came questions about the nutritional value and the potential health hazards of child-targeted cereals. The council's strategy was interpersonal contact rather than petition-oriented, and although it had no formal relationship with petitioning groups, it had a significant role in creating a milieu conducive to that process.[5] In all of these efforts, Saturday morning and its children had been the primary focus of attention.

Surgeon General's Report

Although less directly a Saturday morning focus, the Surgeon General's Report formed another major child-oriented milestone in the 1970s. Twenty-one major research studies had been funded within the landmark project, and the five-volume report of the Surgeon General's Committee was published in 1972. The convergence of research evidence led the committee to conclude that there was a causal relationship between television violence and later aggressive behavior (see chapter 6).

The report had a more profound impact on the research community than it did on commercial television programming. Massive campaigns by the American Medical Association (AMA) and the National Parent-Teacher Association (PTA) produced a notably less violent 1977 program schedule, but the 1978 season bounced back with near record violence levels. Despite its authoritative and pinnacle status, the report had not been a catalyst for long-term changes in programming.[6,7]

Although the Surgeon General's Report had not brought long-range changes in programming, both the report and the violence issue were reaching the public conscience. In 1975, FCC chairman Richard E. Wiley concluded that the evidence was clear enough to justify changes in broadcast industry practices. The method of change, however, was consistent with the FCC position from a few years earlier. Wiley indicated that changes should come voluntarily rather than through the adoption of rigid governmental standards, and he expressed optimism about recent self-regulation initiatives by the National Association of Broadcasters. He was referring to NAB's 1974 decision to overhaul its television code guidelines and cut back Saturday morning advertising time, putting it on a par with adult prime-time guidelines. That same overhaul had banned nonprescription medication and supplemental vitamin advertising on or adjacent to children's programming. Wiley staked his voluntary industry reform position on First Amendment grounds, saying the alternative—governmental censorship—was inconsistent with the freedoms guaranteed within our legal traditions and the Communications Act. "I am certain that the American people do not want a government agency to act as final arbiter of what is or is not appropriate for viewing by their families."[8] But it seemed equally certain that many people were more than uncomfortable with Wiley's position. The seeds of this discomfort were destined to sprout visibly in response to the 1976 program season.

Many people believed that 1976 had been the most violent season in television programming history, matching closely the violence levels of 1967. Even a network president, Robert T. Howard of NBC, admitted, "The proliferation of program types whose plot lines heavily involve violence has become excessive."

Response to the violence trend had been sharp and extensive in several quarters. An already outraged PTA joined the American Medical Association (AMA) in calling for change in the violence programming trend. To underscore its commitment, the PTA held eight nationwide hearings on the issue, and the AMA contributed $25,000 to the National Citizens Committee for Broadcasting to help support a study on television violence. The AMA move, most directly linked to network pocketbooks, was a direct request to ten of the nation's largest television advertisers to withdraw their commercials from the most violent television programming. Two of the firms—Eastman Kodak and General Motors—responded by pulling their advertising. Several others including Sears Roebuck, General Foods, Burger King, and Procter & Gamble supported the trend, and said they would place their advertising very carefully.

With pressure mounting, the networks put out the word to producers that they wanted new scripts to go easy on weaponry, graphic gore, and sadism. Steps were being taken to limit the number of violent programs, and to assure that those remaining were relatively cleansed. The cleansing, however, gave some room for pause. One of the major alternatives was psychological terror and threats. As an off-camera rape or beating was occurring, the viewer would see an on-camera close-up of a woman screaming. This alternative brought little solace to those with violence or child-based concerns.

Producers and writers were unconvinced that cleansing would hold in the area of violence. They knew too much about program history and Nielsen ratings to accept that assessment. They remembered the "clean" action shows that had been canceled (for example, "Kingston: Confidential," and "The Andros Targets"), and they remembered the canceling of the "softer" cop shows such as "The Blue Knight." Then, too, there was the memory of "Hawaii Five-O" and what had happened when its producers toned it down at the onset of a new season, producing what its chief, O'Brien, called "fifteen of the best 'Hawaii Five-O' shows ever." The network's "What have you done?" response resulted in orders to "juice it up." O'Brien followed orders, recalling, "You never saw more blood. In the words of Richard L. Kirschner, CBS Program Practices, "It's a strange animal out there. They [the public] talk out of both sides of their mouths, saying they don't want violence. But they're not buying the shows without it."

Network puzzlement would get passed on to producers who heard the message that they were to write "something that's like a cop show, and sexy, but isn't a cop show" (for example, "Charlie's Angels"). In a world of violence and sexual fantasy, the spotlight turned on the latter, with hopes of good ratings. No one doubted that violence would return to its earlier levels. "No violence, no viewers" seemed almost an industry maxim. Producer Michael Rhodes ("Delvecchio") believed, "No show ever got low ratings because of too much violence." There were other reasons to suspect that violence would intensify again later. Consumer, governmental, and congressional pressure was currently very strong, and it was doubtful that this intensity could be sustained over time. The recent court decision against family viewing on First Amendment grounds, and the current cries of McCarthyism from outraged producers and writers, suggested the off-screen storm might subside and the on-screen storm return.[9] And it did return within the brief space of only one year.

Family Viewing Time

The family viewing time concept lived and died in the decade of the 1970s, and within its short life span it touched many broadcasting realities. One of the foremost concerns of the concept was children. The FCC had been getting heat from Congress—which had been getting heat from its constituencies—to do something about the incidence of violence in prime time. In late 1974 and early 1975, chairman Richard Wiley called in the network heads for several meetings, and from those discussions emerged the family hour concept. Actually two hours in length, the networks were agreeing to make 7 P.M. to 9 P.M. (eastern time) appropriate for family viewing. The agreement also included advisories to alert viewers both during and after the family hour of potentially harmful and offensive material.[10] Scheduled for unveiling in September 1975, the concept was hailed by Congress and the FCC as a good idea. Critics considered it "public relations hype" and "a subtle carte blanche for 'business as usual' or 'gore as before'."

The family hour season proved to be one of the most disastrous ratings seasons in the history of commercial television programming. As early as November, the television critics were calling it the worst television season ever. A prime-time litany of cops and comedy, doctors and lawyers, and dramatic series had opened the season, and only cops and comedy had survived. Just two months into the new season, it was clear that networks were having a meager 11 percent success rate on new programs. Only "Starsky and Hutch" (ABC), "Phyllis" (CBS), and "Joe Forrester" (NBC) had survived in a field of twenty-seven new programs. Prime time at CBS was so desperate that they asked the news department to provide a regular program, and the already successful "60 Minutes" entered prime time in direct competition with NBC's "Wonderful World of Disney" and ABC's "Swiss Family Robinson." Placed in settings such as this, family and children's programs were destined to experience continuing casualties in the ratings game.

With the season's disastrous program failures, the family viewing hour was coming under more careful scrutiny. Questions like "Does America Want It?"

and comments about sexless/bland/censored prime time filled the air. Writers Guild members were considering suing the FCC and the networks for a "conspiracy to violate the First Amendment." Producers such as Norman Lear were furious to see their program successes (for example, "All in the Family") getting time changes due to family viewing. "M*A*S*H" and other leading shows also were under the heat lamp, and angry producers felt both pressured and uncertain about the source of the pressure. Ironically, shows that were riding high—presumably among families as well as the general public—were hardest hit. The networks' heaviest antisex mail seemed to be coming from conservative religious groups and media organizations whereas the violence concern more clearly crossed ideological lines. In both instances, more stringent measures than family viewing were being demanded.

What on the surface had the appearance of a simple, family viewing issue, went deeper and catalyzed nerve centers. In its own way, family viewing had become a repository for frustrations and emotions reaching well beyond its bounds. And into the potpourri came sex, violence, the First Amendment, the Fairness Doctrine, and prophecies of concern about America's personal-moral fabric. Few media concepts would become so massively blessed or cursed.[11]

Sixteen new shows had been christened in family viewing time when it began in September 1975, and only three of them survived into the next season. Had the public literally turned off family viewing? Was the public opposed to the concept and its corresponding television content? Opinion Research Corporation surveyed public opinion at the outset of family viewing and then six months later. Adults favored the concept of family viewing time and supported its continuance. At the six-month polling there was greater awareness of family viewing than when it had started, but fewer parents found the rule helpful in determining what their children watched. The consistent response thread was to continue family viewing. For networks there remained the dilemma of how to improve their disastrous new-show success ratio in family viewing time. A Los Angeles federal judge, meanwhile, had suspended the lawsuit brought by Hollywood writers, producers, actors, and directors against the commercial networks, the FCC, and the NAB. Calling it "utter nonsense to continue," Judge Warren Ferguson asked attorneys to negotiate a solution and meet with him later. With verbal support from viewers and legal support from Judge Ferguson, family viewing headed into its second season.

The fatal blow to family viewing would come in the same court that suspended the writers' lawsuit. In November 1976, Judge Ferguson ruled that the FCC had violated the First Amendment guarantee of free speech and had pressured the networks into adopting the family viewing concept under threat of regulatory action if they failed to comply. Despite strong viewer response in favor of family viewing, the concept was ending. ABC and CBS expressed intent to appeal, and there was some good-faith expression of plans to continue the spirit of the concept, but in the long-range perspective family viewing had ended.[12]

The effect of the family viewing decision on children seemed indirect in 1976, but it had long-term implications. If family viewing no longer characterized the 7 P.M. to 9 P.M. time slot, the parental burdens of monitoring would become much heavier. FCC chairman Wiley expressed that concern in his address to the ACT Symposium in November 1976. He said his real concern was not what the decision said about governmental involvement or what the judge said about his own actions:

> I'll accept my lumps as they come. But I am sincerely concerned about the opinion's effect on the cause of self-regulation. If the decision stands, it may be impossible for the industry to develop any effective reforms on a collective basis. In my judgment, this would be highly unfortunate and counterproductive to our mutual concern for what is best for the children of this country.[13]

What promised to be family viewing's epitaph came from President Carter's nominee as FCC chairman. Charles Ferris was appointed in October 1977, and after a self-imposed, six-month moratorium on public statements, he voiced his positions on the issues. His general theme underscored the importance of marketplace forces, rather than governmental regulation, as the primary shapers and cornerstones of broadcast policy. He subscribed to a concept he termed *zero-based regulation*, examining the current validity of each rule and regulation now on the books and retaining only the relevant ones. He believed the function of a regulatory scheme was to assure that the marketplace forces can work. Specifically on the question of family viewing time, he indirectly expressed nonsupport by saying, "I believe that the end does not justify the means. It's the means that are very, very important—particularly in government."[14] Family viewing was finished.

Prime-Time Access Ruling

The controversial *three-hour rule* was destined to have an indirect but major impact on children's programming. Conceived in 1971 as a means to foster programming diversity, the FCC ruling limited networks to a three-hour "feed" in prime time, handing back to local stations a half-hour of evening prime time. Stations planned various responses to this windfall. Some expanded their dinnertime news hour by thirty minutes; others did less editing and let their movies run two hours instead of ninety minutes; and still others aired public affairs programming or a different local feed program each weeknight in the 7:30 slot. The net effect of the ruling was to create a boon for syndicated programming to fill the half-hours that the FCC had ordered to be local feed within its prime-time access rule.

By 1973, the FCC was well aware that its ruling had not led to the program diversity it had hoped. Planning its graceful retreat from this disaster, in December the commission indicated the networks could have back the hour they had lost on Sunday nights, and they also could reclaim a postdinner half-hour on one of the other six nights if they filled the time slot with children's specials, documentaries, or public service programs.

The bombshell for children came in June 1974. When the FCC relaxed the ruling, giving back 7 P.M. to 8 P.M. (eastern time) on Sundays and a 7:30 half-hour on another night, the syndication companies sued. A U.S. court of appeals decision ruled in favor of the plaintiffs, and requested that the FCC postpone its rule relaxation until September 1975. The suit killed several strong children's program projects on the drawing board. This decision prompted NBC to abandon Saturday morning plans for an hour of news documentaries and children's shows. Likewise, CBS dropped a Saturday morning half-hour of children's programming, and ABC scrapped plans for occasional children's features. Even Disney's 7 P.M. to 8 P.M. Sunday slot was in jeopardy. As many as sixty-five hours of news and children's specials had been planned for early Saturday evenings. The worst tragedy was the scrapped plans for Saturday children's programming that would never be picked up and developed.[15] "Hee Haw," "Lawrence Welk," and other syndicated programming had won a court victory—children had lost.

Children's Saturday Morning Programming in the 1970s

When there are policy rumblings afoot, those whom they affect might be on especially good behavior. Although it is impossible to draw that link directly, the threat of governmental rulings was strong in the minds of television executives, and it seemed likely that they once again would "turn to their children." Whatever their cause or motivation, several of those turnings were very impressive.

A significant Saturday morning first for children in the 1970 season was the advent of "pop-ups." Begun experimentally by NBC-owned stations in New York and Cleveland, the approach was broadened to the entire network on January 23, 1971. The "pop-ups" were educational commercials that used a phonics method to teach vowels, consonants, and sentences. Additional "pop-ups" in math and other subject areas also were planned.

Another notable venture in the "pop-up" tradition came in 1971 as CBS initiated 2½-minute newscasts for children eight times every Saturday, slipping them in at the end of each half-hour of cartooning. More than nine hours of new children's shows also were coming to weekends and their themes had substance. For the first time since 1965, Don Herbert was returning to his role as "Mr. Wizard" (NBC), and Walter Cronkite was anchoring a Saturday morning children's version of "You Are There" (CBS), featuring historic events presented as live-news dramatizations. In addition, the CBS "Children's Film Festival" (Peabody winner) was moving from Sunday to Saturday and was extending to full-season status. NBC would advance in Saturday programming with its new entry ("Take a Giant Step") involving teen discussions of social and personal issues such as family, money, and happiness. NBC's child commitment also extended to weekdays when it planned a Monday through Friday half-hour for three- to six-year-olds. Its balanced educational/entertainment format had an accent on learning. Both on Saturday mornings and on weekdays, the networks were making a truly impressive commitment to children. Although the cartoon/entertainment format was plentiful, the degree of commitment to prosocial/learning themes was virtually unprecedented.

The impressiveness of the 1971 season had been no accident. With the network conscience keenly aware of public and consumer group sentiment, the networks had created a vice-presidency for children's programming. This change was followed by two years of careful planning that included "think tank" resource people from within the industry and conferences with child development authorities. The fruits of this process were unveiled in the Saturday mornings of the 1971 season. Even before it had aired, the season came under heavy attack from citizen action groups, and the barrage gave industry executives second thoughts about well-meaning efforts on behalf of children (see chapter 6). It was an unfortunate coalescence of events that served to dampen industry efforts in prosocial children's programming. In many ways, 1971 promised to be the pivotal year beyond which Saturday morning programming would be predominantly and irreversibly cartoon fare. That fate might have been inevitable in any case, but broadsiding the industry in one of its most conscientious child-centered moments only served to hasten the outcome.[16]

The quality of Saturday morning programming took a distinctly downward turn in 1972 and 1973. Where reform pressures had brought ventures such as ABC's "Curiosity Shop," CBS's "You Are There," and NBC's "Take a Giant Step," these two seasons would move almost exclusively toward cartoons. Many of them were "shrunken adult" programs—animated versions of adult prime-time hits. In 1972, "The Brady Kids" stemmed from "The Brady Bunch"; "The Osmonds" blossomed from the parent show; "Roman Holidays" patterned a Roman family after the "Flintstones"; and "The Barkleys" had a striking, although canine resemblance, to the Archie Bunker family. The 1973 collection of children's versions included NBC's animated "Emergency" and "Star Trek," and ABC's hour of hero-type comic fare. The cartoon cadre was once again closing ranks.[17]

The 1974 season turned warm and human with Waltons spin-offs and an emphasis on characters and relationships, and this tone permeated Saturday morning programming as well. The primary focus was "people shows" and prosocial values. In sheer numbers, cartoons still had their dominance, but now they were playing alongside "Korg: 70,000 B.C." (a cave-people family), "These

Are the Days" (a farm family in the 1800s), "Shazam" (the magic word converting Billy Batson into Captain Marvel, championing those in distress), and "Land of the Lost" (two children and a forest ranger rumbling into a time vortex and discovering a mysterious universe of strange creatures). And even the cartoon programming had its relationship emphasis. For example, "Devlin" featured two brothers and a sister determined to keep their orphan family together.[18]

Saturday morning was center-stage for original and new network programming in the 1975 season. Live-action programs, once thought a second-class substitute for cartoon characters, again were coming to the fore. Space and satire were the "in" themes of the new programming. The space contingent included ABC's "The Lost Saucer," CBS's "Far Out Space Nuts," and NBC's "Return to the Planet of the Apes." "The Lost Saucer" featured two lost bumblers from outer space who mistakenly landed on Earth and generously offered a lift to a young boy and his babysitter. With their predictable penchant for wrong turns, they spent the rest of the season in outer space. The Far Out Space Nuts were a NASA ground crew that accidentally blasted off in a moon rocket. "Return to the Planet of the Apes" was set in 3810 A.D.—a daring move by NBC in the wake of "ape failure" on CBS the previous season.

One of the most significant Saturday morning additions came to CBS. "Shazam" had been a tremendous success the previous season and prompted CBS to introduce a female counterpart, "Isis," in the "Shazam/Isis Hour." Occasionally Captain Marvel or Isis would enlist each other's help in a given program, but generally they were separate half-hour programs, each with a child-based moral or lesson theme that characterized the program's adventure and was summarized briefly at the end by Marvel or Isis. While admittedly "super people," they dealt with very real problems of young people in a sensitive and effective way.

Another serious Saturday morning entry was a family program entitled "Westwind" (NBC), which chronicled a family's sailing ventures through the Hawaiian islands. With dad being a photojournalist and mom being a biologist, their boy and girl teenagers joined child viewers in sharing strong role models, informative adventures, and beautiful underwater film footage.

The satire theme in the season was rampant and set out to spoof virtually anything and everything. "Batman and Robin" came in for their satirical lumps in "The Secret Lives of Waldo Kitty" (NBC); "Mission Impossible" had its comic roasting in "Ghost Busters" (CBS); and the "Odd Couple" became the "Oddball Couple," a sloppy dog and an obsessively clean cat.[19] Amid our laughter, we came to realize how tremendously pervasive the adult prime-time influence was on children's programming. It was an early glimmering of the presold concept that would become all the more prevalent in future children's programming, limiting its creativity.

A note of nostalgia and perhaps renaissance characterized 1975 children's programming beyond Saturday morning. It was like a minirevival of fifties favorites for a new generation of children. NBC had engaged veteran Shari Lewis to host weekday specials for preschoolers once a month. The programs would depict a television station run by puppet chracters and, inevitably, one feature would center on a kangaroo children's show host named Captain Person! "Kukla, Fran, and Ollie" were returning with new material in syndication, and a private New York media service executive, Stanley Moger, had convinced Disney that there was a market for reviving the "Mickey Mouse Club." The market responded quickly and overwhelmingly, encompassing the new generation of Mouseketeers as well as their adult counterparts. When WNEW held a Mickey Mouse coloring contest, it received more than 165,000 colored-entry tear-outs, and clubs were forming on college campuses. Bartenders at popular student pubs wore mouseketeer hats for the 5:00 P.M. viewing session and happy hour. Kids, young and old, were reveling in this flashback to the 1950s.[20]

Nineteen seventy-seven was the next year to hold significance for Saturday morning programming in relation to prime time. The 1976 season brought the miniseries concept to television. Nicknamed "Roots, Jr.," the concept would dramatize a book in perhaps four to ten hours of prime-time television over a one- or two-week period. While network executives saw it as a revolutionary way to relieve their dependence on the weekly series, ABC found within it the opportunity to televise children's novels in its "ABC Weekend Specials." It also provided the format for continuing short-story specials from the previous season and repeats of popular afterschool specials. At the cartoon end of the spectrum, ABC was fielding another first for Saturday mornings—the two-hour program. Featuring fifty Hannah-Barbera cartoon characters, "Scooby's All-Star Laff-a-lympics" would test the cartoon endurance of its young viewers.

Beyond the miniseries concept, there were several specific influences from prime time. NBC was bringing the popularity of Muhammed Ali to Saturday morning with "I Am the Greatest" — "a heavyweight champion of the underdog."[21] Two "Laugh-In" characters were finding their sequels in "Baggy Pants and the Nitwits," and CBS's "Space Academy" featured a young space explorer named Wacko who was something of a spin-off from Monty Python. Beyond prime-time hits, the merchandising fads of the times were having an impact on Saturday morning programming. Skateboards were "in" and CBS combined them with the animal motif to create "The Skatebirds"—a clever twist on a popular sport featuring a pelican, a penguin, and a woodpecker. Merchandising and programming were destined to an even closer Saturday morning relationship in the years ahead as products became the centerpiece for programming with increasing frequency. The sequence from product-to-program meant writers and producers no longer had a blank canvas on which to generate original ideas. The production canvas already had at its center a clearly delineated product to be "written around." In terms of format, the new programming was split rather evenly between live action/adventure and cartoon animals.

Many of the new Saturday morning series had educational and prosocial elements built into them, and each network had its own so-called snippets that aired on the hour or the half-hour. ABC had "Schoolhouse Rock" which taught multiplication and other number skills in creative and fascinating ways. CBS had "In the News," which took an issue of national or international relevance and shared its facets with children. NBC had "Junior Hall of Fame," which had short biographies of children who had made significant contributions to their communities. Health and safety messages also appeared on breaks regularly throughout the morning.

Each network continued and expanded its educational/information snippets in the 1978 season. "Schoolhouse Rock" was being joined by "Science Rock" on ABC, and CBS again featured "In the News." NBC introduced "The Metric Marvels," a cast of metric characters working feverishly for their cause, the metric system. Featured in these two-minute lessons were Meter Man, Wonder Gram, and Super Celsius. Naturally they couldn't resist the temptation to "take me to your liter!"

Beyond the educational/information snippets, the 1978 season looked very cartoon-familiar. The live-action strength of the previous season had faded, and virtually all new Saturday morning programs were cartoon animated. With its two-hour "Scooby" extravaganza in 1977, ABC had discovered the long-term power of a child's attention and an appealing cartoon format. The tremendous success of ABC's experiment led to look-alikes in the 1978 season. "Yogi's Space Race" was NBC's answer to "Scooby," and it too featured several Hanna-Barbera characters. This type of extended cartoon format would prove to have incredible staying power.

Another feature of 1978 programming was the informational format. A shorter version of "60 Minutes" entitled "30 Minutes" was headed for Saturday morning. CBS correspondents, Betsy Aaron and Christopher Glenn, anchored the show and covered a range of subjects including entertainment, sports, science fiction, and problems such as drug abuse. ABC also adopted the informational format within their new weekend show, "Kids Are People, Too." In a sixty- and ninety-minute version—to accommodate local station needs—the approach included music, celebrity guests, information, and an advice column. These program formats along with the snippets were children's informational glimpse on the weekend. Cartoons were still dominant.[22]

There were three distinct features of the 1979 Saturday morning programming—cartoons, prosocial programming, and prosocial/educational snippets. In the cartoon realm, the two-hour extravaganza continued its frenetic pace. Another two-hour superhero program, "The Plasticman Comedy/Adventure Show," was airing on ABC. Other cartoons were resurrecting, prefaced with the word *new*. There were "The New Adventures of Flash Gordon" (NBC), "The New Adventures of Mighty Mouse and Heckle and Jeckle" (CBS).

CBS was encouraging its young viewers to read with "The CBS Library," three one-hour dramas based on contemporary books for young people. CBS also planned to help children understand and accept their handicapped peers with "The Kids on the Block." NBC's "Hot Hero Sandwich" had a music-comedy format that addressed a range of junior high topics from friendship to family to grades, growth, and sex. Although these three shows would be short-lived, they were admirable ventures. "The CBS Library" and "Hot Hero Sandwich" were true classics, yet it was impossible for their ratings to compete with cartoons.

Prosocial/educational messages were alive and well. ABC included thirty seconds of health, nutrition, safety, or consumer information in every half-hour time slot. It also planned a self-initiated cut-back in Saturday morning commercial time in January 1980, and planned to increase the frequency of informational messages. Throughout shows such as "Plasticman," the program leads would take time out to share consumer tips with children, and Dr. Henry's emergency lessons for people (called HELP!) talked with children about first aid. "NBC News" and "NBC Sports" planned six 75-second spots each Saturday under the headings of "Ask NBC News" and "Time Out." Current events were featured on the news side with the sports snippets promoting physical fitness, health, and nutrition. These joined an array of prosocial snippets already in Saturday morning air time. NBC's 1970 venture into "pop-ups" now had blossomed prominently throughout the networks.[23]

Saturday morning terrain carried some very basic contours. Three of the most prominent were cartoon/animation, the influence of adult prime time, and the growth of the informational snippet inserts. Cartoon/animation seemed king. Even in the most live-action/adventure eras, the cartoon format prevailed. Not only did it prevail, but it gave birth to the ninety-minute and two-hour supershows. Adult prime time's influence on Saturday morning was far greater than it had been in any previous decade. The most frequent influence was an animated version of either a show or a well-known star. On occasion, it would be a concept such as the miniseries or the ninety-minute special carried into the Saturday morning context. But by far, the most consistent change was the informational snippet. Some truly creative between-program segments were developed, and the networks seemed committed to continuing that aspect of development. The prosocial appeared far more likely to survive between programs than it did within them. The snippets were not subject to ratings competition. Observers could guess snippets had come as a result of programming concern and governmental pressure, but whatever their motivation, they were successful.

Quality, Ratings, and Children's Programming

Whether commercial television was capable of providing quality children's programming would be resolved "one way or another . . . and soon," said FCC chairman Dean Burch in 1971.[24] Part of the "one way or another" that he envisioned was the removal of children's programming from Nielsen ratings competition. As the decade unfolded, the removal never came. Children's programming on Saturday mornings was just as subject to ratings competition as adult prime time, and in that ratings fray a prosocial or quality program might see daylight briefly, but might soon fade. Burch's early observation had touched a basic irony and hard reality of commercial television. The irony was commercial television's inability to sustain creative, innovative prosocial programming in a ratings milieu. The hard reality was the inevitability of that ratings milieu where profits were the life blood and industry fuel.

The creative program efforts within this commercial television decade were plentiful. Cronkite's "You Are There" (CBS), the "CBS Children's Film Festival," "Take a Giant Step" (NBC), "Mr. Wizard" (NBC), "Curiosity Shop" (ABC), and "Kids Are People, Too" (ABC), were among the many efforts that were creatively inspired with prosocial intent. Their short lives came at the hands of ratings. They could not survive a withering cartoon assault and remain viable commercial program entries. Only the between-program snippets had sufficient ratings amnesty for that kind of survival, and some of those survivors were true creative classics. It seemed clear that ratings put a limit on what could be programmed, limiting quality and content as well. Commercial television's primary role was to entertain for profit. This meant appealing to the mass audience, and experience suggested that the masses were not attracted to prosocial and innovative programming. Commercial television would generally play it "close to the vest," expanding a successful ninety-minute cartoon to two hours, cloning an adult prime-time hit in animation, and so forth. Quality programming in any sense that reached beyond this was perceived as the province of another medium.

An event at the end of the 1970s pointed out the nature and the dilemma of this other medium. "The Wonderful World of Disney" was having its twenty-fifth anniversary in prime-time commercial television while Sesame Street was celebrating its tenth anniversary on public television. Both were pioneering, creative efforts. Disney had come in the early dawn of commercial television with a creative staying power that brought out the child in young and old alike. Timing and innovation had found unprecedented prime-time longevity. A youngster by comparison, Sesame Street had been born and raised in the other medium. No less creative than Disney, it had been passed over by commercial television and spent its life on the Public Broadcasting System (PBS). The notion that a prosocial/educational program—no matter how well-conceived—was a high-risk investment for commercial television was obvious. The province of such programs was deemed to be public television, an entity that just two years earlier on its own tenth anniversary, was described in terms such as *factionalism, fighting,* and *frustration.* Funds were always a problem, but still there was a dream. It was a fantasy that E.B. White had expressed for public television when he said:

Noncommercial television should address itself to the ideal of excellence, not the idea of acceptability. . . . I think television should be the visual counterpart of the literary essay, should arouse our dreams, satisfy our hunger for beauty, take us on journeys, enable us to participate in events, present great drama and music. . . . It should be our Lyceum, our Chautauqua, our Minsky's and our Camelot.[25]

If elements of White's fantasy could be lived on a sustaining basis, they would have to be lived on noncommercial television. As we saw in the 1970s, commercial television could house White's fantasy for only a short time. Longer-term residence was not its province nor its likelihood.

References

1. Barry Cole and Mal Oettinger, *Reluctant Regulators* (Reading, Mass.: Addison-Wesley, 1978), pp. 91–130.

2. Richard K. Doan, "The Doan Report," *TV Guide* (October 2, 1971), p. A-1.

3. Richard P. Adler, "Children's Television Advertising: History of the Issue," in Edward L. Palmer and Aimee Dorr, eds., *Children and the Faces of Television: Teaching, Violence, Selling* (New York: Academic Press, 1980), p. 244.

4. Federal Trade Commission, *Staff Report on Television Advertising to Children* (Washington, D.C.: U.S. Government Printing Office, 1978).

5. Robert B. Choate and Pamela C. Engle, eds., *Edible TV—Your Child and Food Commercials.* Prepared by the Council on Children, Media and Merchandising for the Select Committee on Nutrition and Human Needs, United States Senate (Washington, D.C., U.S. Government Printing Office, 1977).

6. George Gerbner, Larry Gross, Marilyn Jackson-Beeck, Suzanne Jeffries-Fox, and Nancy Signorielli, "Cultural Indicators: Violence Profile No. 9,"*Journal of Communication* 28(3) (1978):176-207.

7. George Gerbner, Larry Gross, Nancy Signorielli, Michael Morgan, and Marilyn Jackson-Beeck, "The Demonstration of Power: Violence Profile No. 10," *Journal of Communication*, 29(3) (1979):177–196.

8. Edith Efron and Neil Nickey, "Violence," *TV Guide* (June 14, 1975), pp. 4–17.

9. Ellen Torgerson, "Violence Takes a Beating," *TV Guide* (June 4, 1977), pp. 6–9.

10. Federal Communications Commission, *Report on the Broadcast of Violent, Indecent, and Obscene Material* (Washington, D.C.: Federal Communications Commission, February, 1975).

11. Edith Efron, "Television After Dark," *TV Guide* (October 25, 1975), pp. 26–32.

12. *Writers Guild of America* v. *FCC* (Washington, D.C.: Federal Supplement, 1976), vol. 423, p. 1064.

13. Richard E. Wiley, Opening Remarks Before the Action for Children's Television's Sixth National Symposium on Children's Television, (Cambridge, Massachusetts, November 22, 1976).

14. Charles D. Ferris, Address Before the New England Broadcasting Association (Boston, Massachusetts, July 21, 1978).

15. Richard K. Doan, "Court Decision Upsets Network Plans for Fall," *TV Guide* (June 29, 1974), p. A-1.

16. Edith Efron, "The Children's Crusade That Failed," *TV Guide* (April 7, 1973), pp. 6–9.

17. Richard K. Doan, "The Doan Report," *TV Guide* (March 24, 1973), p. A-1.

18. "As We See It," *TV Guide* (September 7, 1974), p. A-22.

19. "Daytime," *TV Guide* (September 6, 1975), p. 73.

20. Richard K. Doan, "All Together, Now—M•I•C•K•E•Y . . . ," *TV Guide* (June 21, 1975), pp. A-1, 9-11.

21. "Daytime," *TV Guide* (September 10, 1977), p. 72.

22. "Daytime," *TV Guide* (September 9, 1978), pp. 11, 12-18.

23. "Daytime," *TV Guide* (September 8, 1979), p. 9.

24. Richard K. Doan, "The Doan Report," *TV Guide* (October 2, 1971), p. A-1.

25. Neil Hickey, "Public TV in Turmoil," *TV Guide* (July 23, 1977), p. 10.

4
Winds of Change

Television for children in the eighties found a much colder prevailing wind, and children's issues were viewed in a distinctly different light. A hard-fought presidential election brought Ronald Reagan to the White House in 1980. Some of the key support in Reagan's campaign had come from fundamentalist religious groups and well-organized political conservatives, and President Reagan began a series of cabinet and agency appointments that would sweep over seventies initiatives such as the Surgeon General's Scientific Advisory Committee and the Federal Trade Commission's (FTC) Staff Report on Television Advertising to Children.

An old song quipped, "What's good for General Bullmoose is good for the U.S.A." President Reagan's General Bullmoose was business. Riding the conservative mood of the eighties, Reagan also promoted military defense, deregulation, and fundamentalist religion. Deregulation and conservative religious fervor have been felt directly by television and children.

Deregulation

Two of the most visible ripple effects of deregulation were the end of a rule making and the end of a Captain. The end of a rule making came on September 30, 1981, and brought to a close the major FTC initiative of 1977—its massive volumes of research, evidence, and testimony, and its 350-page staff report. What had been so thoroughly reviewed ended with a deadening brevity. The FTC statement said simply, "It is not in the public interest to continue this proceeding and we hereby give notice of its termination."[1] This statement came as no surprise, yet it dramatized the role of prevailing political winds in the welfare and outcomes of child-related rule makings. The FTC initiative had been a pinnacle effort in the field, endorsed by an unprecedented number and diversity of professional organizations and individuals. There was little incentive for similar future initiatives. An era of grassroots effort and Congressional receptivity had officially ended.

In March 1981, a CBS announcement stated that beginnning on September 28, 1981, "Captain Kangaroo" would be shortened from an hour to a half-hour, and would be moved from its 8 A.M. slot to 7 A.M. For some time, CBS had wanted to expand its morning news, and until this time it had been reluctant to initiate the "Captain Kangaroo" changes. The show's name changed to "Wake Up with the Captain." Linked with the change was a 4 P.M. program in which "CBS News" was required to run a pretaped segment of several minutes in which Bob Keeshan talked about parents and children. As one "CBS News" source stated, "Nobody was thrilled about including Bob Keeshan, but if it meant getting an hour more of news each day, the good outweighed the bad."[2]

There was predictable controversy about the change and the motivations behind it. Keeshan publicly was saying that he wholeheartedly endorsed the new arrangement, noting that on any other network he simply would have been dumped. Here he saw the potential to reach young school-age children at the earlier hour, and he welcomed the chance to "be himself" in the regular afternoon news program. By December 1981, it was clear that Captain's young viewing audience had dropped dramatically with the time change. CBS was saying that it had miscalculated the young child's control over the TV dial at 7 A.M.—a time when household adults were watching the news. There was talk of moving "Wake Up with the Captain" to 6:30 A.M., and CBS's John Rosenfield (Broadcast Group executive vice-president) insisted that the network was not canceling the Captain and reaffirmed its strong commitment to children's programming.

Sources close to Keeshan indicated that there had been only ten-second Sunday morning spots promoting the new show, and while the changes to a 7 A.M. and half-hour show proved unsuccessful, the change to 6:30 A.M. was sure death. One producer commented that both local stations and the networks were now less fearful that the federal government would pressure them to program for children, and Peggy Charren of Action for Children's Television (ACT) saw it as a "don't care" attitude that was detrimental to the welfare of children. In her view, "If broadcasters don't feel threatened by the FCC, they stop thinking of children as an important part of the audience."[3] Whatever the motivation intricacies in this deregulation climate, the bastion of children's weekday commercial television programming was ending.

Fundamentalist Religious Conservatism

Termed "the new 'Holy War' against sex and violence," the focus of religious fundamentalist activism was commercial television. A one-man crusade at first grew into a conservative coalition. Don Wildmon had been pastor of the First United Methodist Church in Southaven, Mississippi. His crusade took root in a late 1970s Christmas season when he and his family were at home. As he sat down to watch TV with his family, "On one channel there was sex. I told my child to change channels. He did. On the second channel there was profanity. I told him to change it again. He did. And on the third network there was violence."[4] Wildmon's anger led to his resigning the Southaven ministry, and organizing church families and friends to conduct TV program monitoring and record instances of offensive sex and profanity. The one-man crusade formally became a coalition in February 1981, with the name Coalition for Better Television.

With 4,000 trained monitors spanning 300 groups nationwide, the coalition included televangelist Jerry Falwell's Moral Majority. The group's instrument was the sponsor boycott, and it regularly publicized in group literature the "Top Sponsors of Sex" and "Top Sponsors of Profanity." The group's impact claims were sizable. It figured that in 1980 alone it had cost the networks $10 million to $15 million in lost advertising revenues. It was impossible to get a clear reading on the impact of the coalition, and response to the coalition was understandably mixed. Network executives were indicating that their sponsors had not been affected and would not be as long as Wildmon was associated with the effort. They believed his own credibility was sufficiently weak, and it would work against the general acceptance and success of his monitoring and boycott initiatives.

ACT distanced itself from the coalition, considering its tactics to be negative and counterproductive, as well as a threat to vital First Amendment freedoms. Similar concerns were voiced by the National Council of Churches and several of its denominational membership groups.[5] The issues reached well beyond the Coalition for Better Television and its founder, Don Wildmon. They reached to the very bedrock of democracy itself. In the recent past, the courts had ruled against family viewing time on grounds that suggested the end did not justify the means, and here again there were questions that encompassed this issue. But the more far-reaching question had to do with the group itself. Did it have the prerogative to set standards of morality and decency in television programming? And if it established those standards, did it have the right to impose the criteria on the general public and the general viewing audience? Once the practice of dictating television content got underway, how far were we from the methods of a dictatorship? What happened to the concept of First Amendment freedoms? The questions were extensive. In the context of conservative fundamentalist fervor, the concerns linked with an equally basic, unsettled feeling about religion-oriented political action committees, and their methods of fund raising and targeting given political candidates in elections.

Censorship was one of the major concerns. The Moral Majority's involvement in the Coalition for Better Television concerned many network executives and viewers. It was not a question of a given group's effort, but it was the more far-reaching principle of charismatic televangelism hyping a constituency for its own moral/religious version of broadcast censorship. Observers felt that the 1981 prime-time schedule strongly reflected Moral Majority concerns, especially regarding sex, and there was growing uneasiness about the power of the move-ment's effect on broadcast freedom.[6] This prompted ABC to take a controver-sial program initiative entitled "Pray TV." Looking at the growing power of politically conservative televangelists, the program focused on the Moral Ma-jority and its leader Jerry Falwell. Examining the electronic church, the pro-gram explored the inherent conflict between a desire to serve the spiritual needs of a worship community and the temptations of electronic power accompany-ing an evangelist's celebrity status. Considered a high-security project, ABC hired extra guards to assure the program's completion and airing.

Isaac Asimov authored an article focusing on the choking grip of censor-ship.[7] He sympathized with the Moral Majority, but felt uncomfortable about self-appointed members tabulating sex points in programming. Believing the general approach could carry with it an oppressive atmosphere that stifled freedom of thought, Asimov looked to history to make his point. He noted that when the sixteenth-century Protestant movement challenged and split ex-isting church structures in western Europe, there were distinct differences in the outcomes, varying by regions and orientations. In some regions a more religiously permissive societal atmosphere had come, whereas in others the forces of orthodoxy had consolidated and cracked down on their opposition. His point was a simple but profound one: where the forces of orthodoxy had prevailed, science, technology, and general creativity advanced least. The epitome of this point was the fierce drive to Nazi orthodoxy in Hitler's Germany, and the net effect of its persecution to drive out freedom of thought and expression, draining off those vital resources to more open, accepting societies. Putting this in the context of the Moral Majority and the coalition forces, Asimov concluded that it might be well to "endure the naughtiness of television and hope that good taste among viewers will eventually prevail" (p. 14). He saw the alternative—setting foot on the path of censorship and suppression—as a path that "if fol-lowed will surely lead to destruction" (p. 14). (For more in-depth treatment of these First Amendment doctrine questions and their implications, see works by Friendly, and Cole and Oettinger.)[8,9]

Sex and Violence: Two Publics and Two Issues

Throughout the history of commercial television there were notable indicators that sex and violence were not the same in the public conscience, and the present issue orientation dramatized this distinction. Dr. William Fore, head of the Com-munication Commission for the National Council of Churches, called it the historic dilemma of television reform. Depending on the orientation of a given reform group, it will center its efforts on sex or violence, but not both. Program-ming in this light is characterized as a two-headed monster. Liberal, progressive organizations aim their swords at the head marked violence, whereas conservative, fundamentalist groups target the head marked sex. In the "magic of the monster," when one of these heads is lopped off, the other grows larger and bolder than before.[10]

Nowhere has the "two headed magic" of violence and sex been seen more vividly than in family viewing time. When 1976 brought one of the most violent programming years on record, the public outcries produced a 1977 season of sex. "Three's Company" and "Charlie's Angels" had Nielsen-ranked in the top four programs, and that strength was not lost as the 1978 season approached. Ratings success for sex-oriented programs brought more look-alikes for the 1978 season. The trend prompted the season to be labeled the year of "kiddy porn" and "jiggle shows."

Critical pitch further heightened with word that six actresses in ABC's planned "The Initiation of Sarah" claimed they had been exploited. They said they were told to wear nothing under robes that would be blown by wind machines. They were embarrassed by the camera's lingering eye on them in humiliating positions, and by the issuance of oversized bras stuffed with foam rubber. Whatever the substance in their claims, the era of Farah Fawcett-Majors as national sex symbol had arrived, and with it a trend in commercial television known as "t & a programming." Ironically the result was not nudity, but a kind of market-share anatomy lesson. If a twenty-second peek down Cheryl Ladd's cleavage on "Charlie's Angels" garnered x number of viewers, would "Wild and Wooly's" three girls in a wooden tub triple the yield? Would Angie Dickinson in her terry-cloth bathrobe on "Police Woman" cancel out Suzanne Somers wrapped in a pink towel on "Three's Company"? The Nielsen ratings verdict was clear. Sex was "in," and violence subsided.

If one viewed the pattern of sex and violence, it would show the two alternately passing each other. When programming became less violent, it became more sex-oriented, and once sex had run its Nielsen course the air would move back to violence. The trend was set by ratings. In a two-network marketplace the second-rated network could still command a profitable and comfortable return on its thirty-second commercials, but this was a three-network arena in which the distance between thirty seconds on the first and third-rated could be as much as $125,000. Within this major league-type competitive arena, the showcase transition between violence and sex went for high stakes.[11,12]

The public that would stuff mailbags against violence was not the same public that would send letters in opposition to sex. The groups, their concerns, and their basic point of origin were vastly different. For example, when Opinion Research Corporation polled viewers on family viewing time, they found the strength of sex and violence concerns varying in different parts of the country. The Midwest had the strongest opposition to sex content, and the Northwest and Northeast had the strongest opposition to violence. The sex/violence distinction also seemed to follow demographic lines. Steiner's classic study of audience attitudes observed two markedly different groups, those who had college training and those who did not. By Steiner's own admission, the distinction was oversimplified, but to the extent that education correlated with broadened perspectives, it seemed valid.[13] The dynamics of the difference would be seen in the present controversy.

The National Council of Churches had studied and taken its cue from the 1972 Surgeon General's Report, and its denominational membership groups had consistently come down harder on television violence as a threat to young children. Fundamentalist conservatives, more literal in their biblical interpretation, found sex most objectionable. Nudity and a basic concept of good and evil accompanied this biblical focus and literalism, making sex a natural target and concern in the television medium. Followers in a fundamentalist tradition were both literal in their biblical tradition and leader-oriented in their commitment to a cause. Denominational memberships within the National Council of Churches, in contrast, were centered within a more scholarly approach to biblical passages—one that studied background and engaged in exegetical work. These differences in point of origin led to equally major differences in approach to commercial television and its issues. Whereas one tradition was more likely to study the evidence, the second was oriented toward applying the values of literally translated scriptural passages to the television arena.

The two publics might soon be of one mind as new programming surfaced on cable television. Some called it "pornovision," and its creator called it a sex-oriented variety show format in the genre of "60 Minutes" with frontal nudity and four-letter words. The program in question was "Midnight Blue," originated by Al Goldstein, whose initial publicity had come with the founding of *Screw* magazine. There were two issues: the show itself and the larger issue of cable television standards and self-policing. In the cable dimension there was an element not present in general commercial broadcasting. Where by owning a television set one could pick up commercial television by turning a switch, one would have to pay to receive cable and programs such as "Midnight Blue." It was a difference between broadcasting and "narrowcasting."

Network executives considered themselves to be at a distinct competitive disadvantage because they were licensed and answerable to the Federal Communications Commission (FCC) while cable television systems were accountable only to the local government bodies that franchised them. Even the television code of the National Association of Broadcasters that encompassed the three commercial networks and most affiliates did not have any cable company members. Cable TV was now pipelining to homes with a directness the networks considered unethical and unfair. The Farrah Fawcett-Majors era of concern that the networks had spawned just a few years earlier now had a much more explicit arena in cable television.

More prevalent and pervasive than a "Midnight Blue" was the tremendous success of Home Box Office (HBO) born in 1972. Starting very modestly on a cable system in Wilkes-Barre, Pennsylvania, it gently expanded to six cable systems and 200,000 subscribers by 1975. Then came satellite distribution. HBO invested $7.5 million in a five-year lease on a satellite transponder, and encouraged cable systems nationwide to purchase the "earth station" antennas necessary for signal reception. By 1981, HBO had over 6 million subscribers in more than 2,500 cable systems, and became an industry standard for a host of imitators. It spanned a program range from culture (Bravo), to adult movies (Escapade and Private Screenings), to movies (The Movie Channel and Home Theater Network), to Spanish-language programming (Galavision). Even the Public Broadcasting System (PBS) was hoping to help its financial status by initiating a "Grand Alliance" of cultural institutions to participate in a pay cable venture called Public Subscriber Network. HBO had come a long way from its modest beginnings in Wilkes-Barre, and in the process began an avalanche of monumental proportions.[14]

The increased competitive pressure on the networks carried direct implications for young viewers. Critics noted that the fifteen prime-time films depicting adolescents in the 1980–1981 season had sexual themes. Among them were "Babysitter" (seduction), "Diary of a Teenage Hitchhiker" (rape), and "Thin Ice" (high school boy's affair with his teacher). The sexiest teenage films (for example, "Fallen Angel") seemed to come during ratings sweeps, and the image of teenage prostitution seemed prominent in ratings sweep selections (for example, ABC's "Off the Minnesota Strip" and NBC's "Alexander: The Other Side of Dawn"). There was growing concern that these made-for-TV movies would not only project the surface and seamy side of sex to adolescents, but they would stereotypically link adolescents with this sex image.[15]

We now gained a clearer perspective on the dilemma of the network executive. Since the early days of competition with the movie houses, the networks felt shackled by their mass audience responsibilities. To compete with the more explicit, the networks resorted to double entendre, innuendo, titillation, and perhaps at times, sex obsession within the program day. Television had been the medium that by its own admission lagged behind the sexual revolution of the sixties. While nudity, intercourse, and childbirth were openly addressed in other media, television permitted "no nudity, frontal, backal or sidal" (Traviesas, NBC). While broadcast standards executives were aware of what was not being permitted, they were also aware that sexual humor and innuendo were virtually everywhere in the programming schedule. Sex may have been out of sight on television, but the compensating leakage was enormous. There was suggestion that our puritanical taboos left us wide open for vicariously sharing the excitement of titillation and subtle reference to "you know what." As one producer characterized it, "You can talk about anything, but don't show it!" In the leakage category, Mike Douglas observed that "There's a great disparity between sex and love, and these days there's more sex than love on the air."[16]

We can see the enormity of the cross pressures. On the one hand, networks were competing not only with one another, but with fast-paced, more explicit, and less regulated media such as HBO. Feeling their mass-audience disadvantage, the networks resorted to humor, suggestion, innuendo, sex-oriented movie themes, and viewer fantasy. Fundamentalist conservative groups, on the other hand, felt outrage and followed their leadership in expressing those views. It was doubtful that either position would fully carry the day, but the tug-of-war unearthed issues that would remain in the air indefinitely. It was doubtful that the public would ever be of one mind on the sex and violence arguments, but it seemed clear from television's history and its present dilemma that these two issues would surface intermittently and strongly.

Surgeon General's Report: The Ten-Year Follow-up

Nineteen eighty-two marked a quiet yet significant year for child-oriented television research. In a difficult political climate the National Institute of Mental Health, through the monumental efforts of Dr. David Pearl, published *Television and Behavior: Ten Years of Scientific Progress and Implications for the Eighties*. It was the ten-year follow-up to the Surgeon General's Scientific Advisory Committee Report of 1972, and summarized an impressive range of research studies relating to children and the television experience. Links in the violence-oriented research chain were stronger and more definitive on the basis of the large volume of research that had occurred in the last ten years. The political climate and public mood, however, were vastly different from their 1972 counterpart, and the report's major reception came from the research community rather than from the public.

In his foreword to the ten-year follow-up, Dr. Herbert Pardes, director of the National Institute of Mental Health, noted that approximately 90 percent of the more than 2,500 research publications on television's influence on behavior had appeared within the past ten years. The report stated that "the evidence for a causal relationship between excessive violence viewing and aggression goes well beyond the preliminary level" (p. 2). The research had broadened dramatically in both the scope of the questions and the range of professional disciplines involved. Most of the effects research centered on children, but the child-related investigations included attentional factors, viewing patterns, cognitive and emotional functioning, imaginative play/prosocial behavior, family/interpersonal relations, physical health, and societal/lifestyle impact. Research had taken a closer look at milieu and longitudinal factors, and the professional disciplines spanned a range that included all the behavioral sciences, most notably psychology, psychiatry, and sociology, as well as public health and communications.[17]

Research support for the causal relationship between viewing televised violence and later aggressive behavior stemmed from what Dr. George Comstock described as "meta-analysis"—the convergence of findings from many studies, the majority of them demonstrating the relationship.[18] In the decade following the surgeon general's 1972 report, the age range in which the relationship had been demonstrated broadened from the original eight- to thirteen-year range to a preschool- to older-adolescent range. Whereas most of the earlier studies indicated that boys, not girls, were affected, the effect had now been shown for both sexes, as well as beyond the borders of the United States.

Two of the basic concerns in the 1972 report—viewing time and program content—had taken on more diverse avenues of inquiry in the ten-year interim. Major strides were made on questions relating to child attention during viewing and level of understanding. The impact of television viewing on the child's emotions also was becoming a topic of inquiry. Researchers were becoming increasingly aware that television viewing had health-related implications for young children. Not only was the activity passive, but it carried within it a litany of lifestyles and habits that were not conducive to good health. Alcohol consumption was common and seatbelts went unbuckled; mental illness was related to violence and victimization. Children who watched television extensively had significantly poorer nutrition habits than those who were light television viewers. Health, nutrition, and their relationship to Saturday morning television ads were central to the follow-up report and its findings, but the significance of the research would be more central to the scholarly community than to the general public. With the exception of occasional news stories on the health and physical condition of our nation's youth, the issues would not lend themselves to quick or easy resolution, if indeed they were resolved at all.[19]

Saturday Morning and Children's Programming

Presold properties, heated ratings competition, and thriving "drop-ins" characterized Saturday mornings in the 1980s. Presold properties were any established or name property that a network or producer could purchase the rights to program. The properties spanned a diverse range, including prime-time television programs and their stars, popular product lines, and classic children's books. Many of each were purchased and programmed in the eighties, and they raised issues relating to creativity and the program development process we will examine more fully in subsequent chapters. More than any previous decade, it was a time to compete for known properties with the strategy and hope of maximizing ratings success. It held built-in tendencies for progressive escalation, and this escalation became especially heated when one network would take the lead and its two trailing competitors would fight ruthlessly to catch up.

Several popular prime-time programs and their stars ranked among the Saturday morning presolds. "Fonz and the Happy Days Gang" boarded a time machine in ABC's 1980 lineup while "The Flintstones Comedy Show" came to NBC. A cartoon version of "Laverne and Shirley" (ABC) joined "Gilligan's Planet," "The Gary Coleman Show," and "The Incredible Hulk" in a bumper crop of prime-time hits during 1981 and 1982. With its familiar story format, "Gilligan's Planet" marooned its cast in outer space rather than on an island, and "The Incredible Hulk" animated its successful prime-time star. The hottest prime-time property was coming in 1983 as "Mr. T" aired in cartoon format. The show brought in the real-life Mr. T at the beginning and end to impart a bit of straight-talk wisdom to young viewers. Another hot property followed in 1984 as Richard Pryor hosted a CBS live-action comedy series called "Pryor's Place." One who served as role model to Eddie Murphy seemed unlikely for the part, but his near-death experience brought with it a commitment to young people, their conflicts, and their future. The show also brought back to children the venerable Krofft puppetry, known to an earlier generation of children in the days of "Puf 'n' Stuf." Names and network hopes continued (for example, "Punky Brewster") as the prime-time stars became increasingly sought.

Idols from children's own prime-time past were in equally strong demand. To land the presold rights to Pink Panther for a new series, "Pink Panther and Sons" (NBC, 1984), was quite a challenge but carried the potential to build on an animated character's beloved status with children. "Muppet Babies" (CBS, 1984) carried a comparable strategy and hope for longevity. The show's goal was to inspire reading. There were many others in this category of the child-familiar from children's programming, and the fight for their property rights was more heated than ever. "The Tom and Jerry Comedy Show" and "The Tarzan/Lone Ranger Adventure Hour" came on board early at CBS (1980). "The Kid Super Power Hour with Shazam" brought animated revival of Captain Marvel and Hero High students. Timeless "Bugs Bunny" completed ten years with CBS and came to ABC as an early-morning newcomer in 1985. If name recognition across generations could carry the ratings, the "Bugs Bunny/Looney Tunes Comedy Hour" could expect a wealth of young viewers. Whether it was adult or children's prime time, and whether animated or live, the chance to purchase name recognition was a bustling enterprise.

An even more bustling enterprise focused on product names and product lines. Product lines were practically crawling all over the Saturday morning schedules, and there was good reason. One of their lines, the Smurfs, took Saturday morning by storm in 1981, and proved virtually invincible against its competition. As NBC gained that Saturday morning edge, the runner-up networks competed. Many of their hopes rode with product names and product lines. ABC bought the rights to "Pac-Man," and aired a show that seemed very much like the plot and setting of the competition. "Pac-Man" held security guard status to "Power Pellet Forest," and needed to constantly contend with villain "Mesmaron" and his quartet of "do-no-goods," Inky, Blinky, Pinky, and

Clyde. Not only were children finding name recognition, but they were finding plot recognition as well.

Soon ABC would also turn to Charlie Brown and Snoopy, Benji, Rubik's Cube, and a popular doll line (The Monchichis). Building on the colorfully frustrating Rubik's cube, "Rubik the Amazing Cube" featured a genie who popped out of his cube and took children on exciting adventures. The Monchichis doll line sent out monkeylike creatures to take on the Gloomies in a cartoon hinterland (1983). On its "Saturday Supercade," CBS featured a quintet of video games, and the board game Dungeons and Dragons challenged its young viewers to solve puzzles and riddles that would enable the show's six children to get back home from fantasyland.

The product-line list carried the intensity of a firestorm. "Dragon's Lair," on the pattern of the arcade game, featured Dirk the Daring venturing into a medieval kingdom (ABC, 1984). The popular game, "Pole Position," brought together a cautious Mustang (Wheels) and a sleek race car (Roadie) as two sophisticated, "high-tech vehicles of justice" (CBS, 1984). The rights to "Star Wars" characters were bought and pressed into service in an "Ewoks/Droids Adventure Hour" (ABC, 1985), and Jim Henson's "Muppet Babies" property branched out into "Muppets, Babies, and Monsters" (CBS, 1985). There was "Alvin and the Chipmunks" (NBC, 1983) and the saga of the Cabbage Patch dolls. The most striking illustration of product-line influence came with the Cabbage Patch dolls. NBC watched wistfully as the Cabbage Patch doll craze swept the nation in 1983. It had purchased the doll rights for program development in 1982, but Hanna-Barbera had found the production assignment difficult at best—a challenge of making the dolls appeal to both boys and girls, along with the problem of translating their orphaned individuality to the television medium. Now that the Cabbage Patch craze had become feverish, so did the price tag for program rights. If NBC did not pursue it once again, CBS or ABC undoubtedly would. The Cabbage Patch saga clearly demonstrated the prevalence of product lines as well as the heated competition for the rights to new, hot product names.[20]

A far less bustling enterprise encompassed the rights to book properties. Although fewer in number, these rights were nonetheless significant. "ABC Weekend Specials" regularly aired book-based dramas, and one of them, *The Littles*, was destined to take on the Smurfs. Based on the best-seller, ABC's two-part special starred the familiar six-inch characters who lived in normal-sized houses. You would be amazed what adventures six-inch characters can have in normal-sized houses! The two-part drama expanded to a regular Saturday morning series in 1983, featuring these tiny humanoids with pointy ears and tails. CBS bought the rights to the *Berenstain Bears*, and developed a show by that name to do battle with the Smurfs in 1985. The cartoon series was centered in woodland Bear Country where a sticky-sweet economy thrived on honey. There were other book-rights markets—some of them children's specials—and such rights were among a network's strategic bets for success on Saturday mornings.

If there ever was hope of a ratings-free Saturday morning, that hope was gone in the eighties. Never had there been a more competitive Saturday morning era, and with it came the escalation seeds that served to choke out a true program production process. As we will discover in subsequent chapters, the strangle-hold of this escalation was prominently experienced at a high-pitched frustration level throughout the production/network communities.

"The Smurfs" provided a classic, laboratory demonstration of what happens when a network pulls a ratings upset and becomes number one. As ABC and CBS drew a bull's-eye over these happy blue trolls, it was natural to think more about overtaking than about programming. One could argue that intense competition brings out the very best, but one might also remember that arousal levels are more effective in their mid-range than at either their lower- or upper-end points.[21] When the high intensity is combined with the fact that enormous investments go into property rights and program episodes, we come to realize that Saturday morning in the 1980s was unveiling the virtual history of commercial television.

It was a history that played sure commercial bets, going with the hot properties and the well-knowns as much as possible, and riding the coat tails of program successes whenever it was feasible. Many of the Smurf ammunition shows hauled out by ABC and CBS bore striking resemblances to their front runner. Early in the push to overtake NBC, CBS aired the "Trollkins." Although they were quick-witted pipsqueaks who rode the trolleys and loved to troller-skate, they were in effect images of the program they sought to overtake. Both by name and description, "The Littles" (ABC) carried equally striking resemblances to the coveted front runner. Copies rarely have the chance of overtaking the original, and in the process of copying, the possibility for a program's own uniqueness becomes threatened. Where NBC could and did successfully copy itself with "The Snorks," the practice promised to be counterproductive when tried by its competitors.

NBC's self-copying had the effect of strengthening and solidifying its number one position. It could further build a format consistency and identification. The introduction of a new breed in 1984, "The Snorks," worked both to build format and create the possibility of longevity. With these Smurf-like underwater creatures leading into "The Smurfs," a stage was set. And three years into its glory there was some chance that "The Smurfs" could fade. If that happened, "The Snorks" might effectively carry that format strength for a while longer.

Front running clearly gave a network several advantages on Saturday morning. Not only could a network solidify its format, but it also could provide the space in which to do creative programming. Once the ratings strength of

"The Smurfs" had been firmly established, episodes provided a vehicle for strong prosocial messages to children. Individual shows dealt with topics ranging from drugs to handicaps, and as a mute Smurf came to their village, the little folks in Smurfdom as well as child viewers, learned the rudiments of sign language. Here the entertainment-oriented and the prosocial found a very natural blend to be admired in the industry for its breadth of topics and its message depth.

There were disadvantages in being the front runner, but the advantages far outweighed them. Producers seldom brought their most promising program ideas to the front runner because they were aware that the network was generally pleased with its schedule. This put the front runner in a position of having to look further and harder for the potentially successful program idea. However, the top network could maintain the strength of its format, whereas the other networks were very likely to lose theirs in the frantic activity of "catch up." As the competing networks try to catch up, they court the risk of losing programming individuality, scrambling their formats, and defeating themselves.

Enjoying its ratings-free environment, the snippets between programs creatively flourished and grew on Saturday mornings. Each of the networks developed several imaginative entries, beaming to its young viewers a diverse range of prosocial/educational messages. Snippets were also called "pop-ups" (NBC's original label), "drop-ins," "mortar messages," "cartoon capsules," and "educational additives." Whatever your name preference they were bright new entries in the window between programs. ABC premiered a new series of brief consumer information messages, "The Dough Nuts," that taught children how to wisely use their "dough." ABC also aired several four-minute drop-ins featuring Menudo, a popular singing group, and Cap'n O.G. Readmore, an animated purring cat encouraging youngsters to "Oh, gee, read more!" CBS's longest-running series, "In the News," had a ten-year track record heading into the eighties.

The strength of these three-minute segments continued, and the networks' news commitment to young viewers took some diverse turns. One of those turns was the addition of an electoral process feature to its "What's It All About?" series. NBC expanded the range of its "Ask NBC News" segments to include 160 questions from children, and Lenny Schultz's skits on "How to Watch TV" were getting six new thirty-second drop-ins. Notable one-minute snippets included NBC's "One to Grow On," in which child idols from adult prime time and the movies (for example, Mr. T and Sarah Purcell) talked informally with young viewers about concerns such as peer pressure and lying. Another sequence of one-minute notables came from an ABC series on how to use computers. Then, of course, there was ABC's all-time classic, "Schoolhouse Rock." In addition to its drop-in sequences, each network produced and aired brief spots on nutrition, health, and safety. Indeed, the snippets between programs dramatically reflected the potential of the ratings-free environment to be creative on behalf of children.

The informational emphasis in Saturday morning's snippets had been influenced by a growing informational interest that networks found within adult prime time. In response to this interest, many adult prime-time projects revealed content reminiscent of a miniseries era. Such eras find congenial traveling companions in documentaries, and both the miniseries and the specials had a strong historical tone. From Alcatraz ("The Rock & Clarence Carnes") to Beulah Land ("Civil War South"), to Vietnam ("A Rumor of War"), to feudal Japan ("Shogun"), a blend of history and drama were coming to the screen. Political docudramas covered a range of topics, including Arkansas school integration, John F. Kennedy's death, Argentina's first lady, and conflict between the Nazi Party and the American Civil Liberties Union in Skokie, Illinois. Mercy killing, the plight of migrant workers and coal miners, and cancer were among the topics addressed in the dramatic forum. The atmosphere was informational, illuminating historical events as well as present day problems and conflicts. Children and their own Saturday morning snippets were the indirect beneficiaries of this atmosphere and orientation.

The growth of news and a general informational emphasis surfaced prominently in the topics addressed within specials. Several topics on ABC Afterschool Specials focused on problems central to young viewers. "Amy and the Angel" dealt with a teenager's attempt to talk a girl out of suicide. "Sometimes I Don't Love My Mother" depicted the struggles of a young girl having to cope with her father's death and the growing dependence of her mother. Two young violinists became romantically involved in "Between Two Loves," and a teen purse snatcher confronted the crime and punishment experience in "But It's Not My Fault." Equally important young people's topics were addressed in the CBS Afternoon Playhouse, CBS Field Trip, and CBS Library. Among Playhouse topics, the effect of a father's unemployment on the family was brought to teen level in "Help Wanted," and "Just Pals" depicted the change in a boy and girl's relationship when they moved into adolescence. On Field Trip "CHIP" star Erik Estrada and Lou Grant's Linda Kelsey took their young viewers on a visit to the worlds of "The Police Officer and the TV Reporter," and CBS Library added "The Wrong Way Kid" to its schedule. For all those adolescents faced with the feeling of never being able to do anything right, these shows conveyed the message that making mistakes was normal. Children and adolescents identified with these programs.[22]

In one instance, there was concern that an informational/issues dramatization had gone too far. The controversial made-for-TV film "The Day After" aired on ABC in 1983, and with its heavy publicity were warnings to parents about its content. The movie centered around a nuclear explosion in Kansas. With the program's fright potential for young children, even Fred Rogers was interviewed on ABC's "Nightline" to counsel parents on how to deal with child-viewing. The film received a 46 national rating (the percentage of all TV homes tuned in), topping the previous record of 36.9 set in 1977 by "Little Ladies of the Night." Hailed as a courageous venture by ABC, "The Day After" had been attentively watched. Many of those attentive eyeballs were young and unseasoned, and there was evidence that the movie's impact had been high, especially among older elementary school viewers. The program and its ratings raised many issues that reached far beyond its content to the effects of such movies on children.[23,24]

Beyond the key features of presolds, competitive pressures, and the growth of snippets, there were other notable characteristics of Saturday morning TV. Both in format and in thematic influences, the 1980s reflected characteristics of the broader social milieu and of adult prime time. The super-show format was once again in evidence, and gave popular cartoon sequences an opportunity to extend beyond typical thirty- or sixty-minute time frames. ABC initiated the super-show concept years earlier, and now NBC was trying it successfully as it extended the length of its star show, "The Smurfs," from sixty to ninety minutes. This extension carried the subtle bonus of throwing off would-be competitor programs that aired on the hour.

On one hand, Saturday morning was themeless, reflecting the clamor of network runners-up to overtake the front runner. As this clamor turned to presold product lines and names, it often represented a diversity rather than a thematic unity. On the other hand, there was the age-old maxim of copying what worked, and as networks copied the "in," they created in an indirect way a kind of thematic atmosphere.

Beyond copying the front runner, there were themes that recurred within Saturday morning programming. When the "hot levels" where low and younger children were the primary audience, small animals, soft cuddlies, or some combination of both seemed virtually indestructible. The 1980s version of the indestructible included "The Kwicky Koala Show" (CBS), "Benji" (CBS), "Alvin and the Chipmunks" (NBC), "Pink Panther and Sons" (NBC), "Muppet Babies," "Berenstain Bears," "Wuzzles" (CBS), and "Zummi, Cubbi, Sunni, and Grammi Gummi" (NBC). Comic books, futuristic settings, and gentle horror creatures also held thematic prominence. ABC's "Richie Rich," its female sequel "Goldie Gold," and goof-up dog "Marmaduke" all were comic-strip related. "Thundarr" (ABC) and "Space Stars" (NBC) were among those tapping the futuristic setting theme, and there were a host of gentle horror creatures including "Dingbat" (ABC), "Godzilla," "Dracula," "Frankenstein," and "Werewolf" (NBC). Either singly or in combination the comic strip, futuristic, and gentle horror were very much a part of the 1980s lineup.[25]

On rare occasions, an adult prime-time hit can create a positive thematic atmosphere that permeates child as well as adult programming. One such occasion took shape in the 1984 season as the "Bill Cosby Show" took on "Magnum P.I." Even in real life, Cosby had never been one to do the expected and the generally accepted. Giving up a Beverly Hills mansion, he moved to a Massachusetts farmhouse. In the height of his comedian fame, he returned to the classroom to get a Ph.D in education. When zero population growth was "in," he and his wife had five children. And now, when everybody knew adults wanted sex and violence, he was bringing TV a family with five children. In a sense, Cosby's own life and family were coming to the screen, and although he would be a success whether the show was or not, one had the sense that this was not just another acting role for Cosby—it was a personal commitment. Many shows had died against the stiff ratings competition of "Magnum P.I.," but Cosby's unique blend of wit, wisdom, and personal commitment prevailed. The show pulled a ratings coup comparable to the Smurfs, and with that coup came a prime-time focus on families and relationships. It was a focus with warm and human dimensions that would support and bolster the tones and elements of Saturday mornings, too. In neither adult nor children's prime time did it mean that violent acts, dynamite, and high-speed cars would vanish, but the Cosby atmosphere was a significant counterbalance.

Role Models for Children—A Time of Transition

In 1984, Captain Kangaroo's morning show for children lost its air slot. After thirty years, recent losses to television news, and time changes, the Captain was leaving. Keeshan's countenance still would be seen on Saturday afternoons as he continued to host CBS Storybreak, a series of specials based on children's literature and designed to whet the youth appetite for reading. The Captain denied that he was retiring, and said that he, Mr. Greenjeans, and the crew would reincarnate on PBS when the time and the funding were right. But for now, at least, an era comparable to that of Buffalo Bob and Howdy was ending, and the partings were similarly quiet and unpretentious. In perhaps a sign of the times, the current idol of children was a prime-time character, Mr. T. "I like Mr. T because he always throws the bad guys out the window," said a Gladwyne, Pennsylvania, elementary school child. Described as mean, cool, and nice, his model was distinctly different from that of Buffalo Bob, the Captain, or Fred Rogers.[26]

As we superimpose the schedule of the 1950s over that of the 1980s, the transition in children's role models takes on a special poignancy. One could easily count eight or ten 1950s role models, and each of them hosted or starred in a program for children. By the 1980s that number had withered to two, and now that the Captain was leaving, there was no such model on commercial television. The lone survivor, Fred Rogers, was on PBS.

The transition picture held several key shades and nuances. In terms of role models and programming, children were losing ground. Whereas once there were many role models within children's programming, now there was only one, and that one was not aired on commercial television. Where the many children's programs and their role models had once been, adult prime-time role models now crossed the threshold. Adult prime-time models were different from their children's program ancestry. The males were macho, and the females were seldom cast in lead roles. The general message of problem resolution by physical aggression had now gained model prominence for the young. Perhaps it was inevitable that children's role models would grow up within commercial television, but the nature of those models left a vastly different message than their forerunners had. To be like them would carve very different profiles and contours than being like those who had hosted or starred in children's programs. They were "mean, cool, and nice," as the child had said of Mr. T. One could only guess how this mix and its difference would translate in a young viewer's life.

With the transition in role models came a change in programming over the decades, especially preschool programming. This change was signaled by the strange mixture of bedfellows who came to the aid of an ailing PBS in the 1980s. With deregulation and PBS's financial troubles there had been the threat and rumor that public television must go commercial for survival. The fact that commercial broadcasters were among the strongest voices in the PBS cheering section did not relate primarily to the felt threat of public television going commercial. Commercial television executives knew that if public television was finished, the burden of unprofitable cultural and educational programming would fall on them. Part of the programming they feared was programming to preschoolers. This aspect of the commercial television schedule had been steadily swept clean over the years and the thought of picking up economic dead weight did not appeal to network executives. With something less than Samaritan motives, commercial television wanted to help public television.[27] Taken in this context, the significance of the Captain's leaving became even more clear.

Role Models for Children—The Lone Survivor

Ironically the 1980s brought with them the twentieth anniversary of a famous trolley line to the land of make believe. The planning stage began in 1954 when Fred Rogers left his floor manager's job at NBC to head for Pittsburgh because he did not like the "violent nonsense" in children's entertainment programming. He went to The Children's Corner at WGED, Pittsburgh. Children's films were intermixed with live banter, and Rogers would sit backstage working with puppets he developed for gap fill-in when brittle films would break. The puppets became personalities such as his majesty the King Friday XIII, shy and timid Daniel Striped Tiger, and pompous and vain Lady Elaine Fairchilde. The show lasted eight years, a time in which Rogers took classes at Pittsburgh Theological Seminary. In 1963, he was ordained a Presbyterian minister with a special ordination charge "to serve children and their families through the media." The following year he went on camera for the first time in a children's series he had been invited to do in Toronto. By 1965, Rogers was back at WGED, and with him came the finishing touches for the trolley line from the "real" living room to the Neighborhood of Make-Believe.

Mister Rogers' Neighborhood was ready for occupancy, and within it young children found a special neighborhood friend who was low key, friendly, and talked to them about a range of tough issues and concerns such as sex, death, divorce, and holocausts—topics many considered forbidden at a young age. His show seemed both behind and ahead of its time. He used none of the fast-paced, state-of-the-art production techniques that soon would characterize "Sesame Street," and nowhere else in television—or in broadcasting, for that matter—could one get away with an entire minute of dead-air silence. But within these paradoxes director Paul Lally commented that Fred Rogers "reaches into kids' souls," and parents such as Peggy Charren (president of ACT) were convinced of this when she heard her young daughter in the next room saying softly, "Mister Rogers? I started school today."

The corporate business community also proved responsive to Fred Rogers. In 1984, Burger King's anti-McDonald's ad campaign used a character named Mister Rodney, asking children if they could say "McFrying." Aware that children were confusing him with the ad character, Fred Rogers called corporate headquarters in Miami. The conversation reportedly was calm, with Rogers asking the senior vice-president about his family, hearing about the executive's young daughter, and so forth. When it was learned that the ad offended Rogers, the company immediately took it off the air with the comment, "The last thing that we want to do is offend you."[28] At his twentieth anniversary, Mister Rogers, his child viewers, and his television future seemed quite alive and thriving. Perhaps one for-children role model was enough. In any event, that is all they had. The transition from the fifties was now complete.

Conclusion

There had been something curiously backward about the impact of deregulation and sex on children in the eighties. In the case of deregulation, where once a children's program spawned products, now the product rights were purchased as the base for creating programs. The change in sequence carried strong implications for program creativity and the issue of host selling. Most producers prefer to start from an idea rather than a product. It gives them a wider canvas on which to develop and create, whereas the product can be an initial constraint that leaves a much more narrow canvas. Both in character development and plot, there is much less opportunity for the broad, sweeping brush stroke. Another "backward" in deregulation stemmed from the accelerated competition in programming. The most creative moments were those couple-minute windows tucked in between regular programs. There was something basically sad about that "backward," but the saddest of all was an exodus in programming for preschoolers. It was not likely that either trend would change.

There was yet another "backward" in the eighties. The action groups that brought the sex issue to the fore were atypical both in process and agenda. Where action groups in the late sixties and seventies worked through governmental agencies, Congress, and consumer groups, this new activism had a vigilante tone to it. On their own, these fundamentalist groups would determine what was appropriate to broadcast and would dictate and boycott accordingly. Although the impact of boycotts seemed short-lived, the new breed of activism and its religious base were very much alive. First Amendment freedoms were in greater danger and jeopardy than they had been at perhaps any time in recent history.

References

1. Federal Trade Commission, Washington, D.C. (September 30, 1981).

2. "Kangaroo Losing Viewers: Will Jump to New Time Slot," *TV Guide* (April 4, 1981), p. A-1.

3. "Kangaroo's Leap Lets CBS Expand Morning News Show," *TV Guide* (December 19, 1981), p. A-1.

4. Ron Powers, "The New 'Holy War' Against Sex and Violence," *TV Guide* (April 18, 1981), p. 6.

5. "The New Right's TV Hit List," *Newsweek* (June 15, 1981), pp. 101–103.

6. "TV Update," *TV Guide* (May 23, 1981), p. A-1.

7. Isaac Asimov, "Censorship: It's a 'Choking Grip,' " *TV Guide* (July 18, 1981), pp. 13–14.

8. Fred Friendly, *The Good Guys, The Bad Guys and the First Amendment: Free Speech vs. Fairness in Broadcasting* (New York: Vintage Books, 1977).

9. Barry Cole and Mal Oettinger, *Reluctant Regulators* (Reading, Mass.: Addison-Wesley, 1978).

10. Powers, "The New 'Holy War' Against Sex and Violence," pp. 6–12.

11. Joyce N. Sprafkin and L. Theresa Silverman, "Physically Intimate and Sexual Behavior on Prime-Time Television 1978–1979," *Journal of Communication* **31** (1) (Winter 1981), pp. 34–40.

12. Max Gunther, "Commercials," *TV Guide* (December 2, 1978), pp. 4–10.

13. Gary A. Steiner, *The People Look at Television* (New York: Alfred A. Knopf, 1963), p. 235.

14. Neil Hickey, "Pay TV vs. Free TV: May the Best Deal Win," *TV Guide* (August 1, 1981), pp. 2–6.

15. *New York Times* (September 14, 1980), p. 38 D.

16. Edith Efron, "TV's Sex Crisis," *TV Guide* (October 18, 1975), pp. 4–8.

17. David Pearl, *Television and Behavior: Ten Years of Scientific Progress and Implications for the Eighties: Volume 1, Summary Report* (Rockville, Md.: U.S.

Department of Health and Human Services, National Institute of Mental Health, 1982), pp. iii–viii, 1–8.

18. George Comstock, "New Emphases in Research on the Effects of Television and Film Violence," in Edward L. Palmer and Aimee Dorr, eds., *Children and the Faces of Television* (New York: Academic Press, 1980), pp. 129–148.

19. Pearl, *Television and Behavior*, pp. 1–5, 9–19.

20. "NBC Fumbles in Cabbage Patch," *TV Guide* (December 1, 1983), p. A-1.

21. Donald O. Hebb, *Psychology*, 3rd ed. (Philadelphia, Pa.: Saunders, 1972), p. 343.

22. "Daytime/New Season/Specials," *TV Guide* (September 13, 1980), pp. 7, 12–14.

23. "Nuclear War: Can We Reduce the Risk?" *Newsweek* (December 5, 1983), pp. 44–48.

24. " 'Day After' Tops Record for TV Films," *TV Guide* (December 3, 1983), p. A-3.

25. Schedules in *New York Times* (September 14, 1980), p. G 13; (September 13, 1981), p. G 13; (September 12, 1982), p. G 13; (September 4, 1983), p. G 5; (September 9, 1984), p. G 13.

26. "I Like Mr. T Because He Always Throws the Bad Guys Out the Window," *TV Guide* (May 5, 1984), pp. 43–45.

27. Neil Hickey, "Public TV: Why Reports of Its Death Seem Premature," *TV Guide* (December 11, 1982), pp. 12–18.

28. Roderick Townley, "He Reaches into Kids' Souls," *TV Guide* (March 23, 1985), pp. 12–14.

5
Television Eras and Children's Issues

E very television era has its milieu, its context, and its issues. The milieu
is the climate of the times. Context is the positioning of an event within
that climate. Where did it occur? What were the immediate conditions
affecting it? Issues stem from events themselves. Were there precedents? What
ethics apply? What are the general implications?

Sometimes the milieu will determine whether a specific event occurs. At
other times, the milieu will determine whether an event is noticed or attended
to when it does occur. Milieu may not rule out an event's occurrence, but it
definitely will affect its perceived importance and value. We see this entire range
of milieu/context/issue interplay within the eras of television and its children.

In many instances, a milieu and its issues are so intricately interwoven that
it becomes impossible to separate them. In other instances, an issue thread can
be seen and traced distinctively throughout every milieu. One such thread has
been society's concern for its children. Natural to any society, this concern was
especially evident in the United States as television came of age.

Context and Concern—A Delicate Balance

The concerns that characterized the 1950s occurred in discrete pockets. With
a general climate of viewer enjoyment, there was little chance for issues to gain
a strong foothold, but there were parents and professionals who were concerned
about the sheer amount of time children spent watching television, and the
effect these hours and their content were having on the young. From no hours
of television to five hours a day by mid-decade was more than a minor change.
It was a basic transformation in lifestyle. To wonder about that change and
its implications was very natural, but the general milieu itself seemed bright
and everyone was basking in it. What faint traces of trouble an observer might
detect were more in the official public sector than in the general public conscience. Neither the National Association of Educational Broadcasters (NAEB)
survey of 1951 nor the Kefauver Committee investigation of television violence

in 1954 triggered the public conscience. Children seemed safe enough and the milieu itself was beautiful and inviting.

This was all to change dramatically, however, in the sixties. President Kennedy's assassination stunned and jarred a public's reverie, and two more assassinations deepened the shock. A reeling public was yet to encounter the Vietnam War and the Kent State tragedy. Violence no longer was distant or pretend. It became central to the milieu.

Two brief decades in television's history had sharply outlined the differential effect a milieu could have on its events and issues. Whereas a Kefauver Committee in the fifties would gain an occasional attentive ear, that same committee in the sixties could have served as the catalyst or springboard to galvanize public concern. To say that milieu was everything might be an overstatement, but one could hardly discount it or give it a minor role. It constituted the vital force in whether an event reverberated or lay quietly in its environment.

An event in a supportive milieu takes on a dominant theme-like character. In the span of the sixties, violence concerns found expression in a senate subcommittee, chaired by Senator Thomas Dodd; in the National Commission on the Causes and Prevention of Violence, chaired by Dr. Milton Eisenhower; in the Senate Subcommittee on Communications, chaired by Senator John Pastore; and in the establishment of the Surgeon General's Scientific Advisory Committee on Television and Social Behavior. All these group efforts occurred within a span of only six years in the sixties.

The thread of public concern in the seventies took a notably different tone. The concern over public televised violence in the sixties had grown from discrete events and shock waves in the general social milieu. The primary vehicles for expressing concern were in the official public sector: senate subcommittees, commissions, and the surgeon general. In the 1970s, television concern became more grassroots. Citizen action groups had more varied elements in their issue focus. They reflected concerns felt by parents and professionals, relating to advertising, its methods, and its products. Young children, it was argued, were a special audience needing media approaches, ethics, and protections appropriate to their age and level of development. The petition, the approach to networks, the commission hearings and notice of rule making, all would be part of this citizen action picture. Although the groups could not gain the full stature of the Surgeon General's Scientific Advisory Committee, its governmental commission milieu, especially that of the Federal Trade Commission (FTC), would be actively attentive. Whereas the concern over violence had primarily taken a research avenue, the advertising concern took a citizen action approach. Each proved heavily dependent on the responsiveness of its milieu and those of political influence within it.

As the thread of concern moved into the eighties, it dramatized how dependent it was on milieu and the political atmosphere. A massive rule-making effort could be dismissed in virtually one sentence from the FTC. The Ten-Year Follow-

Up to the Surgeon General's Report of 1972 could find daylight only through the tireless efforts and determination of Dr. David Pearl at the National Institute of Mental Health. Whereas efforts of this kind would have been encouraged and supported just a few years before, they now encountered an unreceptive milieu. Within the public sector, the concern thread of the eighties had turned distinctly gray. Although still there within the social fabric, it was harder to trace and to follow.

The fundamentalist conservative actions and concerns in the eighties are unique. As they relate to children, they are not an extension of the action-groups that preceded them, and those who pioneered those earlier initiatives cannot join their ranks. Ironically, the starting points for both efforts seemed strikingly similar—a living room television concern triggered citizen activism. But the eighties concern and its activism promoted a religious ideology moreso than an issue, and the group itself closely aligned with the politically cold wind that chilled general progress in children's issues.

Perceived Dangers

A pill bottle sits on the bathroom sink. Is it dangerous to adults? Yes, but adults know it is dangerous, and they know how to use the pills safely. Is it dangerous to young children? Yes, and they lack the awareness of danger and the knowledge of safe usage. How then can the child be protected from that danger, and whose responsibility is it to protect? Should the manufacturer be asked to label the bottle with a "yuk face" or should the company be required to use a container lid that only an adult can open? Should the burden of protection fall predominantly on the parent to teach the child, and to lock up all harmful medications? These kinds of questions surface repeatedly in areas of child protection.

The pill bottle analogy applies in a discussion of television, but it is too simple. Where the pill is the danger within the bottle, the challenge of identifying the dangerous within television becomes more subtle. What is dangerous to children about mere viewing? Who is at risk? Research either commissioned or inspired by the Surgeon General's Inquiry speaks to these questions in relation to violence. Comparable research addresses these questions in the realm of advertising.

A central concern in the violence area has been the question of modeling and imitating. Does a child's viewing of television violence increase the likelihood of that child committing subsequent aggressive acts? Psychologist Albert Bandura's early modeling research in 1963 strongly suggested that children imitate what they see on television, and subsequent research across a range of designs and methodologies generally confirmed the linkage.[1] By the mid-1970s, major foundations were directing their funding efforts beyond the question of violence-viewing effect on children. Foundation members assumed the basic aggression linkage had been established.[2] Other linkages also had been established. As children viewed television violence, they became emotionally desensitized. It was as if they expected what they saw, and developed an accepting attitude toward aggressive behavior.[3,4] There was virtually no support for the early suggestion that violence viewing functioned as an emotional release (catharsis), cleansing the viewer of aggressive tendencies. To the contrary, aggressive tendencies were heightened by viewing.[5]

Two lines of research addressed the more penetrating question of television viewing's long-term effects. Psychologist Monroe Lefkowitz and co-workers found that heavy television viewing in eight-year-old boys was highly related to the likelihood of juvenile delinquency ten years later.[6] Communications researcher, George Gerbner, and co-workers, found that heavy television viewers greatly overestimated the aggression-related dangers in their daily lives and activities. Not only did viewers overestimate dangers, but they also developed expectations of who would be aggressive and who would be their victims. Women, the elderly, minority groups, and the poor were routinely victimized in TV programming.[7]

Since it is impossible to cover the full range of the television-violence debate here, the goal of this discussion is to respond to the violence-programming aspect of what is dangerous. As we have seen, research suggests both short- and long-term dangers—heightened aggressiveness after viewing and cumulative viewing effects relating to desensitization, social fears, and violent/victim perceptions and expectations. Those most notably at risk are young viewers, primarily preschool and early elementary school-age children. It is at this time that viewing patterns form and fears are most acute.[8]

Parents are painfully aware that their children have no comprehension of selling intent in commercials, and parents are regularly begged to purchase products. These concerns have motivated citizen action groups. Barcus outlines the problem areas in terms of time, product types, selling techniques, appeals, and value lessons. When Action for Children's Television (ACT) was getting underway in 1968, ads accounted for almost twenty percent of the time on a Saturday morning schedule. Children saw an average of twenty-six commercial messages per hour. The survey research prompted efforts to reduce the number of messages and the time per hour that could be devoted to commercials. Commercials dropped to an average of fifteen per hour and the time that could be allotted to commercial messages was reduced to 12 minutes on weekdays and 9 1/2 minutes within children's weekend prime time. What happens within those minutes is the essence of product-type, techniques, appeals, and value lessons.[9]

The four major product types advertised to children on Saturday mornings have been toys, cereals, candies, and fast foods. Toys are the dominant motif in the pre-Christmas months of October and November, and research indicates that the toy ads are a primary reference base for children's Christmas requests.[10] These ads routinely lack the basic pricing and general information a buyer would need for wise or comparative shopping.

The food product area has drawn public concern from diverse quarters, a concern prominently focused within the FTC Staff Report on Television Advertising to Children. Several professional groups voiced fears about the dental health risks posed in advertising sugary food to young children. That heavily sugared cereals were virtually the only food group advertised to children was seen as failing to promote the concept of balanced nutrition. Because the ads promoted unhealthful eating habits in their young viewers, they also were considered contributors to obesity. To the Saturday morning child, the world of food was the world of heavily sugared cereal and candies. The dangers of this perception, and the eating patterns it promoted, were viewed as serious by the entire professional health care community.

Host selling was an early technique concern because it identified the child's favorite program personality with a product. It was seen as equally problematic to divert a child's attention from a product by tucking an inexpensive piece of plastic or a trinket inside the box (premium selling). And the practice of using camera zooms and close-ups with an effective soundtrack to make the toy seem fantastic was seen as giving children a false impression of the product. Animated figures interacting with live children and the camera magic of mysterious flights, transformations, and disappearances made the product world one of fantasy for children. Catchy jingles that repeated the product name as often as a dozen times made this fantasy world all the more irresistible for children. When qualifiers, disclaimers, or disclosures were injected into this world, they often were difficult or impossible for the child to understand. If you can imagine yourself as the five-year-old hearing "Partial assembly required," "Batteries not included," or "Items sold separately," you can get a sense of the high altitude these expressions would have as they jet-streamed over your head. Of course, to promote a child's understanding was not the principal goal of these ingredients in advertising messages.

The most frequent advertising appeals to children have been psychological ones. By far, the most prominent message is that of fun and acceptance. Whether verbally stated or visually depicted within the ad, it is a message of how much fun the product will bring and how it will promote the child's acceptance among peers. To the young viewer, this magnetic message is not simply strong, it is exceptionally powerful, especially so when one considers the strength of a young child's need for acceptance. What is lacking in these appeals is "hard" information about the product—its ingredients, its price, its sturdiness, and so forth. Instead, the child hears the words *best* and *great* couched in hedonistic appeals.[11] Barcus notes the poignant tragedy in this singular appeal when one surveys the potential within alternatives such as work activities, education, business, or parent-child relationships.

The value lessons in children's advertising are both straightforward and subtle. Among the straightforward is the hedonistic approach just outlined. The more subtle includes messages about who are the most important people in society. These subtle messages are communicated through the sex role dominance within the ads themselves, the ethnic group representations, and the roles accorded different people in the commercials. Research has consistently found that the announcers in commercials are generally males—generally off-camera, voice-overs. In the few instances where the announcer is female, the products are characteristically household or food-related. Beyond male dominance, the spokespersons are generally adult and white. Character representations within the commercials convey similar messages. Both in role dominance and in product associations, the sex-role differentiations are evident. The ads also communicate messages about important activities. The most prevalent activity settings are leisure ones. Seldom, if ever, is a character depicted in work activity. The connotation of happiness and fun becomes inextricably linked with the setting of leisure.

Child Protection

Having identified dangers both in programming and in commercials, we come to the difficult question of child protection. In a sense, the protection question resembles our encounter with the pill bottle discussed earlier. What are the responsibilities of the various parties contributing to the creation of the bottle and its contents, their marketing, and their placement on the bathroom counter? Whether it be pill bottles or television screens, the parties involved include the product source (in television, the network and the producer), the container manufacturer (those who build and market TV sets), the government (performing a monitoring/regulatory function), and the consumer (in the child instance, the parents or guardians). As we have seen, there are also citizen action groups that perform monitoring functions on behalf of consumers. Even as one begins to enumerate the various constituencies, the complexity of the responsibility questions becomes readily apparent. And as a profit-making enterprise seeks to maximize its return to stockholders, the question of protecting a given group of consumers becomes all the more elusive.

When we find problems in the contents of any container, it is natural to go to the source. In the case of television violence, the source is the networks. They fund pilot programs, and have input on the scripts and their shaping throughout the developmental process. It was early concern about TV violence that led to the formation of *continuity acceptance* departments at the networks, a neutral-sounding term to shield the possibility of these departments being seen as censors. The sections later would be called *broadcast standards*. They have functioned on a case-by-case basis rather than by a general guidelines approach.

A set of general guidelines was stated and subscribed to by members of the National Association of Broadcasters (NAB) in 1961. All the networks held membership in this organization and endorsed the television code guidelines.

These guidelines stated in general terms a special responsibility toward children. In programs designed for children, the broadcasters were encouraged to consider "the range of interests and needs of children from instructional and cultural material to a wide variety of entertainment material." It was felt that the programs in their totality should contribute to "the sound, balanced development of children to help them achieve a sense of the world at large and informed adjustments to their society."

The guidelines expressed special program standards directed specifically toward violence in programming. Physical and psychological violence could be presented only in "responsibly handled contexts," rather than exploitatively, and the program had to present the consequences of violence both to its victims and to its perpetrators. The details of the violence presentation were not to be excessive, gratuitous, or instructional, and the use of violence for its own sake—along with any detailed dwelling on brutality or physical agony—was not permissible. The depiction of conflict in children's programs was to be handled sensitively, and the treatment of criminal activities had to communicate its social and human effects. Questions relating to sensitive handling, whether an incident was gratuitous, what was excessive, and so forth, became the province of broadcast standards within the networks. The guidelines were basic instructions to serve as general rules, with specific instances to be interpreted on a case-by-case basis.

In addition to statements relating to children as a special audience, and treatment of violence in program depictions, the guidelines dealt with specific presentational aspects in several areas including narcotic addiction; demeaning or ridiculing physical/mental afflictions or deformities; sensitivity in program treatment of material relating to sex, race, color, age, creed, religion, and ethnic origin; marriage/family characterizations; liquor/smoking use; and the occult.[12] They constituted the only general set of guidelines subscribed to by all three commercial networks as well as other NAB members. In that sense, they held vital importance.

The NAB Code died an untimely death in 1982. In a civil action suit pitting the *United States of America* v. *National Association of Broadcasters,* the latter lost. The events surrounding the case had little to do with children and their welfare or protection. Filed by the Justice Department under the Sherman Act, the suit charged that the code inflated prices of commercials under sixty seconds because of its limitation on the number of commercial minutes per hour. This was seen as creating a large corporation monopoly on commercial time. The suit sought to restrain the NAB from limiting or restricting the quantity, length, or placement of nonprogram material, or the number of products or services presented within a single nonprogram announcement on broadcast television. When the NAB realized the enormous size of the suits that might be brought against the organization, it reluctantly opted to drop the code. Although the action had nothing to do with violence concerns and children, the guidelines were now gone.[13]

Citizen action groups and related professional groups have joined forces at different points to bring pressure for change. Two notable instances of this in the violence area have been the National Citizens Committee for Broadcasting (NCCB) and the National Coalition on Television Violence (NCTV). The NCCB was founded by Nicholas Johnson, a former FCC Commissioner. Ralph Nader joined Johnson in this effort. The organization regularly has published a *Media Watch Newsletter* in which it ranks the least to most violent prime-time programs on the networks. It also gives the networks a violence ranking on the basis of the violence levels of the programs they have aired. Movies and sponsors also are ranked.

A truly unique feature introduced by Johnson was the concept of the Advertiser Index. Patterned after Dr. George Gerbner's Violence Index, it gave advertisers a rating based on the violence levels of the programs they sponsored. The ten most violent sponsors were given a rank-order listing, and so were the ten least violent sponsors. Johnson's rationale for the approach hinged on the fact that he was dealing with a commercial medium, and that the avenue for change in violence levels within programming would be the pocketbook of the network—revenues from advertising. The chain reaction would begin with the national company whose name had been published as one of the most violent sponsors. The company, in turn, would seek to change the type of publicity it was getting by asking the networks to withdraw its ads from high-violence programs. As these withdrawals occurred, there would be a loss of revenues on those programs which, in turn, would prompt less violent programming. The rationale was perceptive, and had its temporary impact in the initial year it got underway. One network official predicted that since there was only a limited number of programs in the schedule lineup, the sponsors who were withdrawing would soon discover their need to compromise in order to sponsor. Ratings and violence had never been far apart, and it was only a matter of time before sponsors would be returning to the top-rated programs. In this sense, the protective measures were victims of the viewers, a painful reminder that commercial television was a mass medium.[14]

The NCTV is a more recently emerging group than the NCCB. Directed by Dr. Thomas Radecki, a psychiatrist, and based in Champaign, Illinois, the group has a cross-section of professional, church, and concerned citizens among its directors and endorsers. Three times each year, NCTV publishes a newsletter in which it covers TV violence-related news items, focuses on specific issues such as toy and game violence promoted through television advertising, and conducts research reviews. On a somewhat less sophisticated scale than the NCCB, the coalition rates violence in programming as well as in cartoons. Its positions cover a wide range of violence-related concerns, and the group advocates several actions and responsibilities for the FCC. Among them are the requirements, by an act of Congress if necessary, to conduct annual hearings involving producers; to require broadcasters to meet regularly with the public;

to assess the incidence and intensity of violence on TV annually and report its findings to the public; and to study the effect of violence on audience members. The coalition also advocates movie and film rating systems, stockholder actions, public petitions to deny TV license renewals due to excessive violence, boycotts, and prominent church/community involvement and participation at the local levels. While its focus is primarily on television, it also cites research and issues in areas such as video games, rock music, and murder mystery novels, serving catalyst functions for violence. The coalition seeks to raise consciousness, and to focus and channel the response of concerned citizens.

Up to this point, we have been discussing efforts aimed either directly or indirectly at the source of television programming and the potential of changing content and violence levels. Another approach seeks to teach effective consumer skills in the use and the viewing of television. This approach is directed primarily toward families. It is aimed at developing planned and thoughtful use of the television medium, rather than automatic, robotlike consumption. There have been several resources directed toward this goal, ranging in type from multimedia training materials and workshops, to individual articles directed at parents. Built on a strong research base, the approaches hold in common a goal to educate and to inform. Families are encouraged to:

1. make a conscious decision about the role television will have in their lives, deciding what viewing patterns and programs will be compatible with that role;

2. look at the new television season's fall programming schedule for each network and determine which programs are compatible with the household decision;

3. watch with children—a point that research consistently has found to make a major difference in the effects of a viewing experience for the young child;

4. provide alternatives to the television viewing experience;

5. be a model for children's television viewing;

6. support one another in efforts to develop planned and thoughtful use of the television medium.

The approach assumes that any rapid or dramatic changes in TV programming are very unlikely and thoughtful use and consumption are essential. Effective use of television would be essential in any case, but the need for viewer awareness and training becomes even more important in an arena where ratings take priority and violence becomes a norm.

At this point we have said nothing about those who make the container—the pill bottle or the set itself. Their role is a less conspicuous one than either the source or the viewer. We are all familiar with the pill bottle cap intended to be impossible for children to open but proving no small challenge for some adults as well. Such modifications in a container would not occur without concerted effort on the part of consumers and a responsive regulatory climate within Congress and governmental agencies are necessary to protect children. The sequel in television set manufacturing is the channel lock, a device assuring that the channel-searching child cannot tune in a given channel. It is a device that functions on the premise that the child will be alone with the TV, a situation that is not optimal, but is nonetheless frequent.

Advertising carries its own set of child protection concerns. More diverse than program violence, these efforts have had both source and viewer components. Protection concerns at the source have related to all the areas outlined earlier—time, product type, selling technique, appeals, and value lessons. As we noted, tangible progress was made in changing the number of minutes per hour that could be devoted to advertising to children. These regulations place children on a par with adult prime time. With regard to product type, there are given products that cannot be advertised in either adult or children's time periods, notably cigarettes, hard liquor, and firearms. For children, the list also includes vitamins and drug products.

The television code guidelines of the NAB addressed several issues in the selling technique area. Within their general guidelines, children were not to be shown having contact with or demonstrating a product that would be potentially dangerous to them, and broadcasters and advertisers were asked to use special caution in the content and the presentation of ads placed in or near children's programs. Two specific presentational cautions related to host selling and program/commercial separation. No children's program personality was to deliver commercial messages in or adjacent to the program in which that personality regularly appeared, and in programming directed to children under twelve there was to be clear separation of the commercial from the program by an unspecified "appropriate device." In each of these instances, there was a distinction to be made between the guideline and the practice. Both guidelines had remarkably similar intent. The host-selling tenet was geared toward avoiding the likelihood of young children associating their admired program character with adjacent commercials, and the program/commercial separator sought to avoid comparable confusion relating to programs themselves.

In addition to the question of program/commercial separation, the NAB guidelines addressed several aspects of children's advertising, including toys, premiums, food, and snacks/soft drinks. Toy ads were to present the product on its actual merits while guarding against misrepresentation. The guidelines were especially concerned that the toy not be shown in settings that the child was not reasonably capable of reproducing, and there was equal concern regarding the possibility of a child's false impression that everything shown was part of the original purchase. Disclaimers such as "Items sold separately," and "Batteries not included" were required to accompany these toy presentations. Premium offers had both length and presentational provisions, and food ads for cereal products were required to give audio and video reference to the product's role "within the framework of a balanced regimen." Ads for snacks, candy, gum, and soft drinks were not to recommend or suggest indiscriminate or immoderate use.[15]

Since the code had been dropped, sponsors and ad agencies were not technically bound by the provisions, but the nature of those provisions gave evidence of what the Code Authority considered important to children as a special audience. Guidelines generally leave a lot of room for individual interpretation, and the children's advertising guidelines were no exception. Several of those interpretations met the technical requirements of the guidelines, but failed to meet the child's need for understanding. When the various program/commercial separators were tested, for example, they were found to function more as bridges than separators, carrying the child "across the threshold" from program to commercial without accomplishing the desired distinction.[16] Where network separators were used, a child viewer was less likely to know when he or she was seeing a commercial. Consequently, children treated the commercials with the same trust and admiration they brought to program characters. Similar difficulties were found in areas such as balanced breakfast disclosures in cereal ads and disclaimers in toy ads. Although a guideline could be met by "Partial assembly required," for instance, a child's understanding was far better met by "You have to put it together."

The Children's Advertising Review Unit (CARU) at the Council of Better Business Bureaus was organized in 1974, and developed its own set of guidelines for reviewing commercials. Generally working on a case-by-case basis in response to complaints received, the CARU Board continues to meet regularly to discuss matters of policy and specific ads. The CARU is especially concerned with advertising approaches that are likely to mislead the young viewer. It directs its efforts toward ads broadcast in children's programming and other programs where children constitute more than 50 percent of the viewing audience. The targeted age group is children eleven years old and younger.[17]

The organizational efforts outlined focus primarily on advertising time, product types, and selling techniques. Two of the Barcus-cited areas—appeals and value lessons—dramatize the limitations of these efforts. Take, for instance, a product such as Cookie Crisp Cereal. Given the name itself, parents and educators might have justifiable concern since the product name conveys the thought of having cookies for breakfast—not a message or a value most parents want to communicate. Meanwhile, the product has no problem meeting guidelines such as audio and video depictions of the role of the product in a balanced breakfast. The point here is not to single out Cookie Crisp Cereal, per se, but to demonstrate how guidelines can be met while questionable value lessons are being communicated. Associating a product with fun, communicating peer acceptance through the use of the product, and depicting specific settings and lifestyles communicate product appeal.

Beyond consumer group efforts, there is no current organization that addresses advertising values. In that sense, both the violence and advertising milieus become adversarial systems. The advertisers and program producers will push the limits of acceptability. The push places the consumer on the defensive, and by the time a concerted consumer group effort has been mounted, the ad campaign has run its course. If, however, the program content or the ad draw little or no public response, the industry assumes that the limit just tested has met with public acceptability. In subsequent chapters, we will find this limit-testing procedure equated with creativity. Whatever the rationale, it means appeals and value lessons are relatively free, unfettered areas in both their program content and their ad expression. To protect a child in these areas becomes the province of parents, schools, and other socializing agents. The broadcaster/advertiser community takes the position that exposure to these appeals and value lessons is a natural and important part of the child's socialization process, one of the vital steps on the road to becoming a discriminating adult consumer.

Issues relating to sex roles have permeated the content of both programming and advertising, and where women have been the focus of these messages, the tone has been one of traditional stereotype or victim orientation. As communications researcher George Gerbner conducts his annual violence index monitoring of prime time, he consistently finds women to be role-cast as victims, and advertising voice-overs have been predominantly male. As we relate the gender profile more directly to children, we find "the Great Divide." Males dominate the cast of characters, giving them social recognition and status. Sex stereotypes are both blatantly and subtly reinforced, and they serve to enhance the male image and diminish the female. Researcher Bradley Greenberg has said that television's role-casting of women constitutes "one of the most sensitive indicators of the distribution of power and allocation of values that the symbolic world bestows upon its victors and victims."[18] Surveying the top educational shows, media researcher Rita Dohrmann found prominent sex-role inequity. Repeatedly, males were role-cast on the active, masterful side of a relationship whereas females were cast as passive and dependent.

Saturday morning reflects sex-role polarities in which girls and boys have an either/or-type role choice rather than a blending of qualities.[19] Women in the industry experience the counterpart of the Saturday morning programming dilemma. Nowhere do they have program representation equivalent to their numbers, and the Smurfette-type role is more the rule than the exception. It is estimated that women direct only 10 percent of all television production and write less than 20 percent. In 1984, only 6 percent of Paramount's writing staff was comprised of women while MTM Enterprises employed less than 8 percent. No women were writers for two of MTM's major female-character series, "St. Elsewhere" and "Remington Steel." "Cagney & Lacey" has been one of the rare prime-time shows hiring women as writers and producers.

Several hurdles greet women in prime-time's carefully guarded shop. For successful membership application to the Writers Guild of America, West, your resume has to indicate that you have either sold a property or been hired by one of the studios bound by a Writers Guild agreement. In an industry that is proud of its success in debunking social stereotypes, the distribution of writers and producers themselves perpetuates the stereotype.[20]

Women are not unique in their television discrimination problems. Virtually all the groups that Gerbner found to be role-cast as victims are experiencing similar discrimination. Sex-role, race-role, and age-role depictions in television programming and commercials all are vital socialization factors for young viewers. In each instance, the group is under-represented in relation to its actual percentage within the general population. Black and Hispanic characters are generally cast in situation comedies or in criminal roles.[21] This makes the within-industry struggle especially poignant and painful for a black dramatic actor. Less than 5 percent of dramatic roles in prime time and films go to blacks, reflecting in a ratings-conscious industry the belief that minority themes and minority leads in television series spell low Nielsen ratings and disaster. The reality and its tragedy come home starkly to LeVar Burton (Kunte Kinte in "Roots"), who finds himself unemployed and among the most dispensable actors in the business. Equally infrequent is the opportunity blacks and Hispanics have for becoming staff writers on prime-time shows. Like the issues within the general social fabric itself, the role issues within television run painfully deep.[22]

Just as there is no set of guidelines to protect child viewers in areas such as program/advertising appeals and values, there is no set of guidelines to protect child viewers from inequities in role portrayals. As protection becomes an impossibility, the hope for creative, prosocial programming initiatives becomes central. Most initiatives in children's prosocial programming have occurred within public television. It is here that young viewers find their "Sesame Street" and "Mister Rogers," and it is here that programming is not tied closely to ad revenues and Nielsen ratings. Prosocial initiatives within commercial television occur as notable crosscurrents rather than the normal flow, and as some of them succeed in the Nielsens, they create hope for others. "Cagney & Lacey," the "Bill Cosby Show," and "Golden Girls" have been among the crosscurrents in prime time. Each challenged a stereotype. It will take similar successful challenges in the future to draw traditional role messages away from their accustomed moorings. Nowhere is this challenge more vital than within children's programming.

References

1. Albert Bandura, Dorothea Ross, and Sheila A. Ross, "Imitation of Film-Mediated Aggressive Models," *Journal of Abnormal and Social Psychology,* **67** (1963):601–607.

2. Eli A. Rubinstein, "Television Violence: A Historical Perspective," in Edward L. Palmer and Aimee Door, eds., *Children and the Faces of Television* (New York: Academic Press, 1980), p. 121.

3. Margaret H. Thomas, Robert W. Horton, Elaine C. Lippincott, and Ronald S. Drabman, "Desensitization to Portrayals of Real-life Aggression as a Function of Exposure to Television Violence," *Journal of Personality and Social Psychology,* **35** (1977):450–458.

4. Joseph R. Dominick and Bradley S. Greenberg, "Attitudes Toward Violence: The Interaction of Television Exposure, Family Attitudes, and Social Class," in George A. Comstock and Eli A. Rubinstein, eds., *Television and Social Behavior,* vol. 3 (Washington, D.C.: U.S. Government Printing Office, 1972) pp. 314–335.

5. Victor B. Cline, Roger G. Croft, and Steven Courrier, "Desensitization of Children to Television Violence," *Journal of Personality and Social Psychology,* 27 (1973):360–365.

6. Monroe M. Lefkowitz, Leonard D. Eron, Leopold O. Walder, and L. Rowell Huesmann, *Growing Up to Be Violent: A Longitudinal Study of the Development of Aggression* (New York: Pergamon, 1977).

7. George Gerbner, Larry Gross, Marilyn Jackson-Beeck, Suzanne Jeffries-Fox, and Nancy Signorielli, "Cultural Indicators: Violence Profile No. 9," *Journal of Communication,* **28**(3) (1978):176–207.

8. Edward L. Palmer, Anne B. Hockett, and Walter W. Dean, "The Television Family and Children's Fright Reactions," *Journal of Family Issues,* **4**(2) (June 1983):279–292.

9. F. Earle Barcus, "The Nature of Television Advertising to Children," in Edward L. Palmer and Aimee Dorr, eds., *Children and the Faces of Television: Teaching, Violence, Selling* (New York: Academic Press, 1980), pp. 273–285.

10. Andre Caron and Scott Ward, "Gift Decisions by Kids and Parents," *Journal of Advertising Research,* **15**(4) (August 1975):15–20.

11. Barcus, "Nature of Television Advertising," p. 281.

12. The Television Code, Code Authority (Washington, D.C.: National Association of Broadcasters), pp. 3–7.

13. United States District Court for the District of Columbia, *United States of America* v. *National Association of Broadcasters,* Civil Action No. 79-1549, Final Judgment, Filed November 23, 1982.

14. *Media Watch,* Newsletter of the National Citizens Committee for Broadcasting, P.O. Box 12038, Washington, D.C. 20005.

15. The Television Code, pp. 12–14.

16. Edward L. Palmer and Cynthia N. McDowell, Program/Commercial Separators in Children's Television Programming, *Journal of Communication,* **29**(3) (Summer 1979):197–201.

17. Robert B. Choate, "The Politics of Change," in Edward L. Palmer and Aimee Dorr, eds., *Children and the Faces of Television: Teaching, Violence, Selling* (New York: Academic Press, 1980), pp. 323–338.

18. Bradley Greenberg and Thomas R. Gordon, "Social Class and Racial Differences in Children's Perceptions of Television Violence," in George A. Comstock and Eli A. Rubinstein, eds., *Television and Social Behavior,* vol. 5 (Washington, D.C.: U.S. Government Printing Office, 1972), pp. 185–221.

19. Rita Dohrmann, "A Gender Profile of Children's Educational TV," *Journal of Communication,* **25**(4) (Autumn 1975):56–65.

20. Michael Leahy and Wallis Annenberg, "Discrimination in Hollywood: How Bad Is It?" *TV Guide* (October 13, 1984), pp. 6–14.

21. Pilar Baptista-Fernandez and Bradley S. Greenberg, "The Context, Characteristics, and Communication Behavior of Blacks on Television," in Bradley S. Greenberg, ed., *Life on Television* (Norwood, N.J.: Ablex Publishing Corp., 1980), pp. 13–21.

22. Leahy and Annenberg, "Discrimination in Hollywood," pp. 6–14.

Part II
The Programming Terrain

6
The Program Development Process

Like the depths of a sea or the layers of a massive rock formation, Saturday morning program development has many layers, complexions, and nuances. In its most fundamental terms the calendar surface of children's program development is September/October, January/February, March/April, and the first week of September. The program development season begins in September as production houses bring their program ideas to the networks. These ideas come in very general, shopping-list-type form as the production house and the network seek common ground. It is a bit like my bringing you a list of ten or eleven models that I have thought about. You look at the list and say, "I really like this one. I'd like it better, though, if you made these modifications and made the lead character gentler." If the network is sufficiently impressed with the idea, it will buy a development option. In effect, the network buys the right to that idea during development and is asking the production house to fill in the skeletal image with personality and character structure.

Once the network buys the option, story and artistic development get underway. At each step of the process, the network has the opportunity to review and modify the series bible, a written description that lays out characters, their individual personalities, their relationships to other characters, and so forth. Once the bible and models are approved, the artist will draw up a couple of set-ups—artwork that will show the characters in particular situations with some quick references to what they are doing. Next the writers take a story outline and, once approved, go to script. Meanwhile, the network takes the artwork and does focus group tests with children. Once the testing is in and the script is in, the story idea goes in the hopper with all the other shows that have gone through the same process and will be vying for series status in the coming season. As one producer said, "We take a character and try to give it personality. We work with relationships and we start development right along their lines." Once in the hopper, it is a case where many are called but few are chosen. If the story idea is fortunate enough to be among the chosen, the network will write a series contract with the production house in March or April.

The bible and basic artwork are the cornerstones of development. The bible gives a detailed description of the series and its format. The personality of each character is highlighted and described. For example, in the bible of "Fat Albert and the Cosby Kids," Dumb Donald's description says:

> He lives up to his name in every way, from the foolish stocking cap he wears pulled down over his face to wearing the right shoe on the wrong foot. But he is good-hearted, and if he comes across anyone in need, Donald will gladly give him the shirt off his front! He is the master of the malaprop but his totally unconventional approach to living proves to be a Godsend at times, because he comes up with the right answer, out of left field.

Fat Albert's description says:

> Undisputed leader of the gang. He is big, loveable and the perennial optimist. Despite his great size and strength, he is very sensitive. He will go to great lengths to help a friend (or stranger!). Fat Albert's inherent sense of right and wrong often allows him to come up with the needed solution to a problem. He is the conscience of the gang but is no "goody two-shoes." When the chips are down Fat Albert is brave and few bullys would tangle with him. He is very bright and aware that the gang sometimes takes advantage of him but after all, "What are friends for?"[1]

The bible continues in this manner, introducing the entire range of characters from Weird Harold to Rudy to Mushmouth to Fat Albert's mom and dad. In a way, it is like getting to know each family member and their friends intimately. Not only does it set the stage for introducing dialogue and series themes, but it gives network executives and new writers a frame of reference that will enable them to gain rapid familiarity and a natural ease in working with the program series. The bible also contains sample dialogue with camera angles and character activity noted.

Prospective individual program themes are presented in one-sentence, synopsis form. Again, pertaining to the *Fat Albert Bible,* a few typical synopses would be:

> *Lying.* Edward, a friend of Fat Albert and the gang, learns a hard lesson about telling the truth.

> *Creativity.* The famous junk yard band is organized when the kids are unable to afford musical instruments.

> *Moving.* Fat Albert goes through the trauma of moving to a new neighborhood.

> *Four Eyes.* The kids help one of their friends to accept the fact that there is no shame in wearing glasses.

The Newcomer. Dumb Donald goes through a tough adjustment when his parents have the nerve to foist a little sister on him.

Tomboy. One of Fat Albert's little girl friends learns there is nothing wrong in girls being interested in what are considered "rough sports".

Mom or Pop. The gang are exposed to the heartbreak of divorce.

Little Business. The kids get suckered into a get-rich-not-so-quick scheme. They are in for a shock when they realize they have been taken. They learn to look before they leap.

Whereas each of these focuses on a basic conflict encountered by young people, the themes in commercial program development are generally less prosocial and more singularly entertainment directed. Producers see the overall format as one in which good triumphs over evil, a framework that spans the entire gamut of programming from cartoons to action/adventure to fantasy. In fact, it is a framework so general that it includes virtually any media story-telling to any television-viewing age group. Artwork is created to accompany the bible. Main characters and some of their characteristic settings are drawn.

Depending on the type of option sales year a production house has had at the networks a house could have a very slow or a frantically busy development season. One production house may have obtained development option on two or three ideas for any given network, and sales at each of the networks are quite likely as well. For a production company having a successful network sales year the development season could be a multiple program-idea development time with its own set of pacing and juggling challenges.

During the development season, the network will have regular involvement with the process. The degree of involvement will depend on numerous factors, among them the track record of the production house, the network's past experience with the producer, how controversial the program or its main character may be, and how much feedback the production house may seek at different points in the process. The natural aim of both production house and network is to create a program that will be engaging to children and will sell. Selling in this instance means attracting children to that specific network for that given hour of Saturday morning programming.

When the development options and their accompanying bibles and artwork are submitted to the network in January, program characters are then child tested in different focus group settings, using the storyboard-type format and accompanying descriptions. The programs that fare well in the testing will remain in consideration for the coming season, and the testing may provide basis for modifying given aspects of the format or characters.

Network broadcast standards executives will begin their review work with a program very early in the development process. Children's programming executives are eager to have broadcast standards input early to avoid any potential standards snags that may arise later. Since there is no written set of standards guidelines for the producers to follow, this early review becomes especially critical. In one of the familiar scenarios, children's programming will alert standards to a development property that they are especially interested in. Standards will review the preliminary materials submitted and will inform programming of any potential problems they see at that stage. They will continue to review as the project develops, communicating directly to the producers any weaknesses or difficulties they are finding within the bible or script. Standards functions independently of children's programming at all the networks, and on occasion the "stereophonic sound" a producer receives from programming and standards respectively can spawn frustration and confusion. Generally, though, the working relationship between standards and programming executives is a congenial and close one.

Networks have diverse patterns of advisory panel or consultant involvement within the review process. NBC has the Social Science Advisory Panel of authorities in the field of child development. This panel meets periodically and discusses a range of issues from the very general program types and approaches to very specific recommendations relating to program characters, scripts, and topic treatments. Seldom does the panel have major impact on a program buy, but it frequently has major influence on the characteristics and the shaping of individual programs. One notable example of this shaping occurred in relation to the "Smurfs." One of the writers for the program suggested a program on the topic of death. The thought immediately raised red flags among the executive staff because the staff considered the topic problematic and inappropriate for the young child audience. Before making a judgment on the idea, staff members took it to the Social Science Advisory Panel and were told that it would be entirely appropriate if handled with child sensitivity. Naturally the expertise of the advisory panel was sought in details of program development, and the net effect was an outstanding program and an Emmy Award for the "Smurfs" series.

ABC has an ongoing advisory relationship with Bank Street College of Education in New York. Child development authorities at Bank Street review every program script and make recommendations prior to airing. Again, the input is prominently at the program series level rather than at the program buy level. CBS functions primarily on an individual consultant basis. It has regular consultants that have been retained by the network over several years, and it engages the services of other professionals as questions arise in given program-related areas. CBS perhaps has the most individual approach among the three networks. One aspect of consistency across the networks is the point at which most advisory input occurs. Only in a rare case would the input be "pre-buy," and virtually never would it determine a program buy.

Network program schedule decisions are usually made in March, but sometimes as late as April. In many instances, the final decisions will not be development options that the network bought the previous fall. The late decision making gives production houses a very tight, frenetic schedule to meet air deadlines in September. This crunch becomes especially real in the case of animated formats. The sequence in animation is a step-by-step process, much like an assembly line that has to be followed sequentially to assure that the first program completes the "line" by its September air date. At that point, the second program will be near completion, and so forth.

A new program adoption may be combined with a summer movie release to introduce children to the characters and format, facilitating their habit of program viewing in the fall. This type of combination was done effectively in the case of the "Muppet Babies," introducing children to the stars and getting them accustomed to the idea that the Muppets had babies. The movie/program concept was not strikingly new. Several cartoon characters had made their debut in movie theaters long before they appeared on the television screen, but in those instances the movie generally had not been created for the purpose of promoting television program success.

When a calendar cycle is completed, children greet the fall program schedule and begin their channel selection voting on an hour-by-hour basis. Like an incumbent running for re-election, the network with the success record and identifiable star characters from the preceding season has a desirable position-edge heading into the new race. The network likely will have both continuity and momentum. If it has cornered key time slots, it will plan its intermediate-slot programming as a bridge, anticipating that the child will "stay tuned." The process looks simple in basic calendar terms. However, hardly a layer beneath the surface, a different world of pressures comes into focus. Without the fullness of this different world, the calendar itself becomes deceptively naive.

Program Selection

The program development process is not without its problems. If you were to ask producers and network executives what they see as the major weakness within the program selection process, the consistent answer would be "Time!" There are two key dimensions to the time problem. Time means producing quality programming by air date. It is this aspect of the problem that most producers and executives have in mind when they refer to it. Time also means selecting the programming that the network schedule needs.

The problem of meeting air date is an annual plague to producers and networks alike. It stems from some of the deadline realities of the program development process. Development options are bought by the network in late September or early October. The artwork and bible are back in network hands in January or February. Artwork is child-tested in January, February, and sometimes as late as March. If the program decision is not made until May, as is often the case, the production schedule is strictly a wall-to-wall, flat-out crunch. Pulling out all the stops and folding thirty hours into each twenty-four hour day, the production house will perform the miracle of meeting the September deadline.

A comfortable production schedule would be five months, but the more usual production schedule is four. Within that crunch everyone loses. Producers feel as though their supplier tails are being heavily stepped on and they have no room for thoughts of creativity and quality. Children's programming executives live on edge that the air date schedule may not be met. Broadcast standards executives find rough cut coming in on the program too late to make changes, a factor which could veto airing but rarely does. No one within this crunch feels able to do their job well, and the frustration has a grinding effect on producers and network executives.

Part of the air date problem stems from the "hot property" dilemma. In March, near the time when networks are finalizing their schedule decisions, each production house will rush to the network with its "hot property." It may be a property option obtained on a doll, a prime-time show, a children's book character, a rock music star, or some other property that might have a significant child attraction factor. Meanwhile, networks may be engaged in much the same activity, seeing what property they might obtain to upstage their competition. There are several tragic elements in this scene. Development options that were virtually in the new programming schedule will be scrapped in favor of a "hot property." Several months of intensive development effort at the production house will be tossed aside in favor of a property that is virtually undeveloped. There will be no development time possible on the "hot property." A schedule and a decision-making process that could have some pacing and rhythm to it becomes a flurry of last-minute run-ins.

The dynamics of this process are poignantly known by all participants, and over time a deliberate practice of developing the mediocre occurs. For example, a producer has several ideas in mind for a given network. The producer knows that any idea submitted early may be nosed out by a last minute run-in, so instead of submitting the best one or two ideas early, they are held for the March run-in. The ideas that get developed are not the best, and the producer's best may be a shoo-in even though the idea is undeveloped.

No one likes the net effect of this process or the near ulcer moments it brings, but the producers feel powerless. Within the program option period there is no chance for secrecy regarding what is being developed at each of the networks. Writers form their own informal communication network, so the proposed schedules and developed properties are known throughout the production houses. "Hot properties" become the vehicle of surprise with the intent of gaining competitive edge. Even the schedule may be juggled at the last minute to catch another network off guard. Pressure, surprise, frustration, tragedy—all part of a pervasive, sticky web that seems ill-equipped to serve either the development needs of the industry or the quality needs of its consumers.

Time as it relates to the point in the fall programming season where decisions are made about the next year's schedule can be illustrated in two brief vignettes. In the first you are the children's programming executive at the network that ranked third in the previous season. You naturally want to find the strengths and weaknesses in your current schedule, and make intelligent decisions regarding your program needs and how best to meet them. But you are assessing your needs in the fourth quarter of the ratings year—October through December—when the current season's programming has just gotten underway. Since you were ranked third the previous season, the strengths and weaknesses in your current schedule will not become evident until the children have seen everything on the other two networks and are tuning in your schedule. This tuning pattern will not happen until the end of the fourth quarter. By then you have to be making programming decisions, and it is decision-making time before children have reviewed and, in effect, voted on your present schedule.

In the second vignette, you are the children's programming executive at the first-ranking network in the previous season. You want to spot the weaknesses in your schedule early enough to do something about them in your planning for the next season. But since you rank first, your shows dominate among viewers during the fourth quarter, and children will be watching your schedule. At about the end of the fourth quarter, your child viewers will begin to look at the other networks in the time slots where they consider your programming weak. Your decisions about the weak spots will be guesswork at best. The child-ratings data will not yet be in to help you.

The two vignettes point up another reason why networks tend to delay their decision making. Although a network may have a pattern of testing new program concepts in January, it may instead test them in February or March. In addition to surprise, the late decision making can have the advantage of further data regarding viewer-perceived weak spots, but timewise that data comes at a very high price to all participants. It leads to network comments like, "I think we'll get on the air. I think the production company will do everything it can to get on the air. I'm pretty sure they'll make it. I'm not absolutely sure, but almost." In this two-fold sense, time is the problem . . . time is the enemy.

Other aspects of time further complicate the process. One network executive expressed regret that there was not enough time to sit down and work with the writers.

> I took home ten scripts last night to read and several outlines—all are shows—and I got through about half of them last night and I really didn't get a chance to go back and read them twice. This is every day. I have ten more plus the five I didn't finish last night to do tonight, and it just keeps going like that. And that's a problem. I perceive my job to be a superstory editor . . . to develop characters and story. . . . I don't have time to work on each script individually. I don't think the production companies do either.

Because of the time pressure and the convenience of New York and Los Angeles, most of the child testing goes on in these two locations. Some children's programming executives wish for the time to do testing in more diverse locations such as the Midwest. "That's where the true heart of your audience is. New York and Los Angeles kids are more sophisticated than I care to see them."

Broadcast regulation executives find their own problems within the time factor. Even though they have reviewed bible, script, and artwork, they have no opportunity to see the proposed final product until the rough-cut stage. Quite frequently, the time period between rough cut and air date is too short. For instance, it would not be unheard of for standards executives to see rough cut on Friday for a show that is to air the following Monday. One can readily understand the lament of one standards executive who said, "It's too late to make changes if there are problems, and there frequently are." And in the view of another standards executive, "Some of the production houses are notoriously bad in their promises to make changes."

Producers find many weaknesses in the program development process that reach well beyond the time problem. The head of one production house believes the biggest weakness is the lack of any tenure or job security for the network executive. It means the executive is unlikely to support an original concept submitted by a production house. Network executives cannot afford to take the risk of supporting an original concept. Their job insecurity also means that they have to think of their career prospects beyond the executive position. Where will they go? With whom will they find employment? They must continually be thinking of where their next move might be. So in the revolving doors of this small village they think, "I'd better be nice to Production Houses X, Y, and Z because I'll be looking for future employment among them."

A related problem is creativity. As one production house chief stated, "I wish we'd get back to designing original characters with longevity and personality . . . which is not really around at this time." Already we have seen several elements that weigh against the creative original program, such as network executive job insecurity, time pressure, and the market-safe haven of the presold. Chapter 10 will discuss in detail the dilemma of originality and creativity in a commercial marketplace.

Producer/Network Relationship

The group of production houses supplying Saturday morning programming is relatively small. Typically six or seven houses produce the programming for any given season. These houses vary in size and there are newcomers. The largest house is Hanna-Barbera. The originator of animation techniques for Saturday morning TV, it parented "Ruff and Reddy," "Yogi Bear," "Scooby-Doo," "The Flintstones," and a stellar list of other cartoon friends children know and love.

Ruby-Spears is smaller and, for its size, carries a heavy Saturday morning program schedule. These two come under the same corporate umbrella of Taft Broadcasting. Filmation, within the corporate realm of Group W (Westinghouse), is perhaps best known as the originator of "Fat Albert and the Cosby Kids." "He Man, Masters of the Universe" has been one of its recent ventures into the videocassette market. It is the only production house that does all steps of program production "in house." The other houses send their program production work to facilities abroad.

Marvel is one of the newer, smaller houses. Headed by a progressive, well-respected woman executive who got her experience at two networks and Hanna-Barbera, Marvel is seen as part of the "new wave" and the future of children's programming. Another potential ingredient in that future comes in the form of DIC. Luxembourg-based and new to the American market, it sold four programs in the 1984–1985 Saturday morning schedule. A Japanese firm, TMS, joined DIC as a newcomer and entered the 1984–1985 schedule with a Fred Silverman production ("Broots") for ABC. Even as you read this, the letters on the Saturday morning production lineup may have changed. Filmendez and Children's Television Workshop, for instance, are likely to become more familiar on Saturday morning.

Seldom will a house leave the ranks of prime-time production to enter Saturday morning programming. In the 1984–1985 season, Krofft Productions did it to initiate a comedy hour approach hosted by well-known personality, Richard Pryor. Because of Pryor's past in X-rated humor, the market entry drew considerable controversy as a children's program. No one, however, questioned the creativity of Marty Krofft and his brilliant track record in both children's program production and prime time. His unique background in puppetry, and his own family history of having been born into show business, held for some the thought that he, too, might pioneer and shape the children's programming future.

It is natural to wonder whether producers are treated as equals by the networks. Can we assume that the small production house stands on an equal footing with the large house when program buys are considered? Statistics suggest fair treatment. Forty-four percent of the 1984–1985 schedule was programming being developed by small production houses. If Ruby Spears is removed from that group and the statistic pertains to programming that went to newcomers, the figure is 22 percent. A significant portion of the schedule is contributed by the small as well as the small-and-new.

Producers believe the small production house receives equal treatment. As the head of one small house explained, the networks want to assure diversity among suppliers. In a group that already is small, the networks do not want to be dependent on the one or two large corporate entities without any realistic prospect of market competition. The networks want small houses to succeed. The prospect of competition within a market has further implications. Whereas the large corporation might become lethargic or somewhat indifferent if it was the major or sole source of network supply, the presence of smaller houses prevents that malaise from happening. Painful as it is to acknowledge in a year when their own sales are low, even the large production houses will admit that the presence of the smaller houses is good for them, too.

Small size brings with it some predictable advantages and disadvantages. The network receives more personal attention from the small house, since it needs the network business to survive. Networks are likely to have chief executive interaction with the small production house, whereas mid- or lower-level executive interaction might be the more frequent pattern at the larger house. This is a definite plus for the network, and a potential problem for the small house. As one producer said, "We give more personal treatment and we hustle more because we're hungrier." When hunger blends with the stark reality of survival, some of the small houses may strike deals that are not in their long-term best interest.

Joe Barbera tells of when he and his fledgling group set out to bring animation into the television industry in 1957. "Everybody looked at you in horror and said, 'We can't afford animation in television!' because we were averaging between $45,000 and $65,000 for five minutes. So to get into the business we took a deal that gave us $2,700 for five minutes. That's what you call ingenuity." It may be what you call disaster for the small house today. The temptation of hunger may be to render personal service at a lower cost, but the small house cannot survive on that Spartan diet. As one production house chief said, "On the social level the smaller house may get more TLC but in deal making the small independent can be very much beaten up."

From the network perspective the smaller house also has a lot to prove. It is not an entirely unknown quantity to the network. There are individuals within the smaller house who have a proven track record and the respect of the network. Small houses often hire a well-known producer to enhance their network credibility. So the unknown letters TMS will have the known Fred Silverman. The untested DIC will have the well-tested John Schalopson. Saying Marvel will become equivalent to saying Margaret Loesch, and so on. The letters and the company name may be new, but the company, per se, is not unknown. Like the tendency to identify children's programming departments with the network executives who head them, production houses become identified with individuals, too.

For winning network confidence, track records are important. The network wants the assurance that the lesser-known production house can deliver the programming, and that assurance comes through the known personalities working with the lesser-known house. If both the personalities and the house were unknown, it is doubtful that a new production house venture could win the support of the network and its business.

Among the children's programming houses, there are some who want to move in the direction of prime time. Their track record is impressive, but it is a record gained within the children's programming market. The familiar network response to this aspiration is, "But you have no experience in prime time." One could say that the network is keeping these production houses tracked where they currently are. Only one producer, Marty Krofft, has been able to move freely between these two worlds. His successful puppeteering history and his life as part of a well-known show-business family add a rare collection of elements to his record. For most production houses the track has more rigidity.

Fortunately, there are few houses looking for cross-overs. They are committed to the children's programming market. For many it seems to be the appeal of being childlike and, in a way, "with children." In the words of one producer, "You never age in this business. Everyone runs around being kids—you know, making jokes and hiding." Many houses have no desire to "grow up" to prime time. On the other hand, they frequently bring prime time back into the children's market, buying a prime-time program option and developing it in animation. So for many the track, though rigid, is not confining.

The currency of the production track record is important. If a production house has something going that is working, that house will have a better shot at getting something else going. As one production house chief said, "Yesterday's hits don't buy you too much."

References

1. "Fat Albert and the Cosby Kids," *Fat Albert Bible* (Reseda, Calif.: Filmation Studios, 1981), pp. 15–16.

7
The Producer

When the word *producer* comes to mind, it inevitably brings with it images of the deep tan, the mirror glasses, the director's chair, the expensive casual outfit, and a Hollywood movie set, or perhaps on-location in the Caribbean. Seldom do we think of concrete buildings on a crowded, narrow street with newly hung curtains, in quarters that have just been rented for a new series contract. But the latter picture is far more characteristic than the former. Although a few major production houses have locations and offices of long-standing, the smaller and newer houses rent as they can and move to larger or to less expensive quarters as the year, the market, and their needs dictate. Glamor and childlike dreams of the producer's world are quickly tempered by the realities of their settings—a seasonal business with good years and bad years, creative dreams and realistic frustrations.

Producer Profile and Child Development Background

The professionals in the production industry are as diverse as the industry itself. They range in age from thirty to sixty-five. Some of them have spent just a few years in children's production and others have spent as many as forty years. If we were profiling the "median," we would find a producer who is forty-three years old and has been in the business sixteen years. The producer is likely to be "he," and "he" is likely to have the B.A. degree. His major could span a large spectrum, but art would be the likely front runner. He may or may not have had any course background in child development—the pattern is mixed but leans more toward no courses or training. Both those who have had courses in the field and those without child development background feel it is not important to their production work. Although one producer told me that a child development background is a blessing, that view was in the distinct minority.

There are several reasons why producers consider a background in child development to be unimportant. As one producer said, children's programming is an entertainment medium, oriented toward delivering a product. The primary requirements are an artistic background and "a feel for what kids like—a natural, gut instinct." This instinct is clearly seen as being "born, not made," and in that context there is little, if anything, the child development background can add. Talent is seen as the key, and producers believe the best environment for developing that talent is industry work experience and not the classroom. They see the advanced degree as losing time. "The sooner you get into a studio and learn reality, the quicker you advance." Entertainment skill, talent, and instinct appear to be the major qualities producers see as important to industry hopefuls. If producers have any child development-type questions, they prefer to handle them on a professional consultant basis, much as they would any other areas of issue-related inquiry.

Chief executives within the production companies have even stronger views on the child development issue than those of their producers. One of the most successful among them has a strong psychology background, and says he finds it totally irrelevant. If he were retracing his college degree steps, he would now major in English, since he sees sense of story as the basic preparation one needs for success in the business. As another chief executive said, "A good story is a good story. A good piece of entertainment is a good piece of entertainment." If a producer has that sense of entertainment and talent for story, there is little the chief executives would suggest adding in any formal, academic sense. "Young people have to have a talent. They have to grow up into the business. I don't think there's a school."

Producer Backgrounds

Unlike the astronaut or the doctor image, most producers did not set out as children to find their careers and fortunes in the TV industry. A few grew up in the industry and just assumed that it would be their livelihood. Another handful pursued TV because of their interest in art, animation, and cartoons. Although they may not have selected the business, per se, it became a natural extension and expression of interests they had. For the largest group, however, TV was more a case of happenstance—needing a job and coming to the industry in search of work. Timing and happenstance, perseverance, and opportunity doors opening in the wake of ability provided the largest group of producers with employment. There are a few producers who grew up with television from its infancy. They are a select, senior group who have known the industry from its fledgling beginnings. It is with this elite group, and its unique perspectives on television's early years, that we will begin looking at the different roads to careers in production.

Growing Up with Television

Lou Scheimer is the founder and president of Filmation Studios.

I went to art school. I graduated from what was then Carnegie Tech. And I came out here in 1955 hoping to get a job in the animation industry. And basically to get a job in the animation industry you're talking about programming for young people . . . and it was the heyday of the animation industry. It was when UPA was going in a valuable studio doing terrific stuff. And unfortunately it also was the end of the animation industry as it was then known because just about that time was when the majors were starting to close their animation studios. Warner Bros. closed theirs shortly after that—I worked at Warner Bros. in 1957. I guess around 1958 they shut their animation studio. MGM closed their animation studio in the late 1950s. Disney had really stopped making shorts in the late fifties, early sixties. I have no idea when they did their last short—"Mickey Mouse." And television had really not started to pick up the pieces. I mean, the animation studios that exist now basically exist for television. And when I first came on, unfortunately the majors were shutting down and television had not really started. And the only thing around was doing animation for commercials. And there were a bunch of studios around that fortunately kept the animation industry alive in those early days doing commercials. But it was not until, I guess, the early sixties that television really started to become significant. Hanna-Barbera came in 1957, and they were doing their first series for television with a show called "Ruff and Reddy." And it was a syndicated show—I think perhaps Kellogg sponsored it, I can't remember. In those early days sponsors really were buying shows and placing them and bartering them and hiking back time and stuff like that. But it wasn't until the very early sixties that television really became important with network television. I guess it was really H and B [Hanna-Barbera] that broke into it with the Flintstones. That was a nighttime show, and there was a bunch of stuff after that. When I started the studio . . . it was in 1962. The first three or four years were dreadful . . . I mean, a lot of the time we were on the toilet! [Laughs.] We'd pick up a job every now and then, but it was difficult. But in 1965 we sold the first network show. Actually, we didn't sell it . . . a national periodical, the comic book company, sold the show called "Superman." It was long and involved, but they came to us to produce it and that literally started us in the networks, so our first show on the networks was 1966. And from then on . . . we've done something. We did lots and lots of stuff . . . 2,000 half hours, I guess, or close to it . . . I have no idea right now. Over the years lots and lots of series.

Another perspective on the early years is that of Art Scott, vice president of special projects at Hanna-Barbera. He, too, had gone to art school. Scott remembers the struggles of those early days:

I was with Disney for nine years. I was with television for twenty-two or twenty-three years, and even prior to that I was with live television when it first went on the air, somewhere around 1948 or 1949. I was with a show called "Cyclone Malone." I helped design the characters on the show, and then started to work the puppets . . . and was doing some voices. . . . So I was really in it from that standpoint from almost the beginning of television. Television came to town here (LA) in 1947. Somewhere in April KTLA really launched the first commercial television in Southern California. The only other station in town was W6XAO which was top of the hill over here which was owned by Don Lee then. They weren't commercial at that time. Then they gradually moved into commercial broadcasting. But KTLA really opened the doors to Southern California for television.

I had no particular ambition that I can ever remember. I went to UCLA and while I was there I studied art and got a teaching degree at the same time. 'Course in those days you couldn't get a degree in art. You had to have it in something more practical, so education was the other branch that tied in with it. So that's how I finally got out with a degree. But while I was there I met an animator, working at the old Charles Mitch Studios which did "Scrappy Cartoons" and "Crazy Cats." And prior to that I had tried once in a while to write to Disney and get some information about possibly starting there working in the summer time, and I always got a negative response from them. I wrote a script and submitted it to Warner Bros. one summer and they offered me a job, but when I told them I was going back to school in the fall they said, "Forget it." In the meantime I met this other fellow who was working at the Mitch Studio and he taught me the rudimentary principles of animation. With that as a background I proceeded to get into the business because he had a job waiting for me when I got out of UCLA. I think I graduated on a Sunday and went to work on a Monday for the magnificent sum of $16 a week. Guys hashing in the local drugstores were making a lot more. I'd been working at Penneys in a part-time job and made a lot more money than that. But you used to sit there and draw and say, "Wow, they're payin' me for this . . . just sitting and drawing these dumb little drawings!" Beginning from there I had no idea where I was going in the business because unless you get some broad background of animation which wasn't being taught in those days . . . there was no such thing in schools as an animation class. That was all some mysterious "never never land" out there. But fortunately I had taken every kind of art work I could get my grubby fingers on, and that was mechanical drawing, life drawing, sculpturing, making jewelry, studying the old masters in art in order to get through and fill up my time. And it all held me in good stead as years went on, as I found out later, but I had no idea what good it was going to be at the time. Usually you would say, "This is a dumb course, what do I need this for?" Well, as it turns out, there were no dumb courses . . . students, maybe, but the courses all had something practical if you paid any attention to them. Thank goodness they've all been of some help along the way.

Born into the Industry

Those who were born into the industry may have had family backgrounds on the show business or the production side of the picture, and the migration toward production was a predictable one. They knew the industry and they knew its tools, and they found it very natural to work within the world they had lived so intimately throughout their early years. The flavor of this avenue and its experience can be found in these accounts:

> I grew up in the animation industry so it's just an extension for me. It's sort of like your father owns a garage so you work in a garage. I always saw myself getting involved and continuing those relationships.

> My family's always been in television. This has been an ambition of mine ever since I was a kid. I've been exposed at some level or another all my life.

> I've been in it forever. My father was in it so I'd work in it after school. That was 1939, 1940, so I've been in it just as long as I can remember. I've been in it for a long time in all capacities . . . messenger boy, casting office, production manager, film editor primarily, then from that to directing and writing and producing. Writing was always an ambition. The motion pictures were not that strong. My father was in it. I was not overcome with the glamor of it. I saw that it was a merciless business. But it was a means to an end. It was a means to go to work quickly, and it certainly was a good thing. So I've been here since then.

> My entire family has been in show business all my life. I grew up with puppetry and appeared on stage with Judy Garland and other stars when I was just a kid.

Pursuing an Interest

Those who had an interest that bloomed within production likely came to the area through art or communications. Each route is described within the following:

> Out of college I was an art major, and I had made some films. But that was just an extension of the art I was doing at the time, because art was my interest. I went to college in the sixties, and film-was-art and art-was-film. So I did that as an extension of painting. When I got out of college I went to the TV station to try to find a job in their commercial art department. I had a background in film, and I thought I knew television and film and how to relate it to the graphics there. They said, "Well, we don't have a job in the art department but we're working up a commercial production department, and I see you've shot some film, would you want to do that?" And I said, "Why not!" So I did that. And I made more films, and I worked in commercials and wrote commercials, directed commercials, and produced them. And then I'm also a magician—had been doing that since I was a kid—and they knew about that. This is a thirtieth size market—Louisville, Kentucky—and they needed a person to host a kid's show at the time because around 1973 the FCC was leaning on them to do local children's programming for the good of the community. So in order to satisfy that FCC obligation they had a locally produced children's show, and I produced and hosted it . . . did magic and things.

So that's how I got started in children's television. And then from there I went to Atlanta, producing a children's film series which was distributed throughout the South. So then I left there and said, "Well I'm going to try Los Angeles." I came out here and fortunately, I guess, got a job with a network, in ABC Children's Programs because that was my background. I didn't consciously go into children's. It's an area I liked, but there were a lot of open doors into that area. I just fell into it and just grew from there. Now I guess if I wanted to get out it would be more difficult to get out because I have this background in it. And I don't really want to get out . . . not now. But I'd like to do some prime time.

I went through communications school. As an undergraduate I was working at a station in Philadelphia. So it just evolved. It wasn't a life-long ambition. I wasn't a child of television, watching and feeling like I just had to be in the television business. It just happened that way. And it's fun.

I had a couple art courses but basically had no schooling. It was always an ambition of mine. I just had worked in the business and had an instinct for it and learned the craft from working.

Happenstance

There was not even a hint that production would be in the future of some. They set out to find a job, and they found production.

Not at all [my career ambition]. I was trained in liberal arts, pre-law, graduate school in government, community relations, a change I had made to labor relations. And then I went in the brokerage business originally. And I wanted to change career fields. I just didn't feel suited. And I really don't even know how I got in the brokerage business other than needing a job when I finished school. But one thing you find out—as you know—is that when you have a basically liberal arts background you really can't do anything! [Laughs.] So I came out to this part of the country only because I had family friends and saw it as a place to interview for various types of jobs. And I interviewed with the three television networks. Although I had been a singer all through school and had performed in theater and little theater, I always viewed that as a luxury and not something that would be a career. I started with ABC as a typist.

This woman went on to an executive position at NBC and major involvement with the success of the "Smurfs." After another executive position at Hanna-Barbera, she proceeded to head a production company.
    Said others:

I've never had ambitions. I've sort of fallen into every step I've taken. And it's always been a move up and always been a move forward. I don't have a master plan and I never did. I started out at NBC in 1974 as a secretary in the children's programming department. And about a year and a half or two years later there was an opening in management and I was promoted by my superior (who was at that time Margaret Loesch), who had been with Hanna-Barbera and now is at Marvel. And in 1979, I guess it was, I had an offer from Warner Bros. TV in the children's division. It was during the Silverman era at NBC and there was a lot of craziness going on, and I at that time was manager of children's over there. And I left there to go to Warner Bros., worked in their cartoon department and headed that cartoon department in 1980–1981. And after a couple years there—Friz Freleng was there and we were doing some compilation features with the old Warner Bros. product—we had decided that we were basically going to stop production and just work on the library or the occasional special projects. Margaret had been after me for a couple of years to come over to H-B and help her out and I took advantage of that. So I've been here at H-B for a year. Producing was not always an ambition of mine. I always wanted to go home at six. [Laughs.] I don't do that any more but [laughs] that was my ambition.

I just seem to have fallen into this sort of position. When I started I had no idea I would end up in an animation studio. It was just the luck of the draw and who would hire me when I was looking for work.

Perspectives for Aspiring Producers

Erikson spoke of generativity as the mid-life capacity to reach beyond oneself toward those who will follow after. As producers make these reflections and speak openly to younger hopefuls, there are several key aspects of their message. Perseverance, preparation, and talent surely rank as the cornerstones within their thoughts to the young.

We think of perseverance as a key ingredient of success in any field, but it seems especially so here. In the words of a legend:

Keep at it. You can't expect to be given everything. You will have to earn it. If you write and draw it will help you. If you really want it you can't give up. TV is a spotty business. Mid-November to April 1 there are lay-offs. Take training classes at night. Put 'em to work if you can. Keep goin'. If you can draw, fine; animate something on your own. You never age in this business. Everyone runs around being kids.

The perseverance message comes through repeatedly as producers give advice.

What matters is perseverance and not talent. Keep knocking at the door and eventually it will open—either by luck or by your own stamina.

Expect to work hard and do everything that comes your way. That's how things happen . . . sweep floors, and so forth.

The important things are perseverance and attitude. Somebody comes in bright, energetic, and doesn't have a chip on their shoulder . . . you can move pretty quickly in the first level.

I would advise them to get their schooling in—four years of college, no matter the major . . . then get into the business and start at the bottom. I had twenty-five students from majors at Loyola. They had a great attitude. They started as runners for me. One is ready to be an associate producer; another, a director. It's a very difficult business. There are the disappointments of ideas and efforts that don't happen and then there are those that do.

My advice to a young person is to do it. The glib thing to say is stay out of it. Inevitably some of them would get very successful. There are tremendously talented young people. A young person can anticipate mostly frustration. Some measure of them will get to do what they want to do. A performer would find it impossible. [It's] toughest [for] somebody who wants to produce. A skill that's marketable is a hell of a lot better off. Writing is the best craft for marketability. It's such a wonderful ability. If you can write comedy, sooner or later you'll make it.

Preparation is a mixed picture. There are tools one can bring to the industry that will be very helpful, notably writing/storytelling skill, and perhaps art. But too much preparation—case in point, the graduate degree—is seen as a loss of time. Experience within the industry and the first-hand involvement with that on-site education is a high priority.

English skills are critical. Get a good background. Work on the ability to speak clearly and write clearly, along with whatever is needed to polish and hone those skills.

Develop writing skills. There are a lot of cross-overs—producers that were former editors, editors that were former producers.

Entertainer Role/Teacher Role

Do producers think of themselves as teachers? Quite clearly they do not. They openly admit that their role is to entertain. As one of the leading producers said:

I don't pretend to be a teacher. I'm an entertainer. I see nothing wrong with it. I don't apologize for it. We set an example . . . we're not teaching . . . we're entertaining. We do teach one of the very basics—the difference between right and wrong—and it's better to be good than bad. Kids have to have their time to be entertained.

Other producers reflect that children get teaching five days a week in school, and are ready to be entertained on Saturday morning. One remembers wistfully his own childhood experience with the Saturday afternoon matinee movie in his small hometown theater: a time to unwind from the week at school, a time to get away from the books and the daily experience of homework and such, a time to be entertained. TV as an occasional inspirer to read or to explore is great. When a theme such as "Beauty and the Beast" or "Thundar" is featured, for instance, children are found to read more about nature. Producers view these outcomes pleasurably as desirable byproducts of their work. It is clear to producers, though, that TV has other purposes. As one producer said:

> Children have to know that this stuff exists in the world—that people get hit, that not everyone is nice, that people get hurt, and so forth.

Selling a program that entertains is the producers' understandable top priority. They are in the business because they know intimately the art of entertainment and how to appeal to children. In their business, teaching is not a profitable enterprise. They see teaching as the province of the Public Broadcasting System (PBS) and the classroom. The Children's Television Workshop model of bringing entertainment and teaching together effectively is not a model that producers consider tenable for commercial television. Although some nurture their creative fantasies about ideal Saturday morning programming, they see their reality as keeping abreast of fads and trends, and incorporating them into a captivating update of the Saturday afternoon matinee.

Self-Identity and Network Identity

Producers view themselves as creative professionals in the child entertainment industry. They know how to make children laugh. They know what is fun for children, and over the years they have created the characters that children of all ages know and love. Producers have pride in their accomplishments, and with that pride comes a desire to be recognized and appreciated by the networks as creative professionals. Unfortunately producers feel as though they are supplier/servants for the networks.

Several facets of the producer-network relationship spawn the servant image. Imagine that you are a producer who has spent twenty-five years in the children's television entertainment business. Your name is known and revered throughout the production industry, and your accomplishments over the years have been acclaimed. It is now program development time in a new children's television season, and you have submitted an idea to the networks. Young people who have come to the network from a nonproduction or nonentertainment background review your idea, and tell you that it is ineffective and will not work. They may also tell you that the cartoon character sketch you have submitted has the wrong type of eyes and they should be redrawn in a certain way. The frustration and the hurt felt by producers in moments such as this are very natural and understandable. The profound depth of that hurt comes home poignantly when younger producers express—with tears in their eyes— how a virtual legend in the industry has been treated on a given occasion by a network. Producers want network respect as the accomplished entertainment professionals their experience and track record affirm them to be. They want to be acknowledged as creative entertainment specialists who can help the network become effectively and creatively entertaining to children.

Ideal Children's Programming

Like many of us, producers have a wistful, faraway look when they think about ideal programming for children. And after that relished, momentary pause, one finds prominent evidence that they have thought about and wished for many of the program opportunities they are expressing. Among producers' ideal program perceptions, one theme is doing creative sequels to the classics (for example, sequels to "The Time Machine," and "Alice in Wonderland"). Within the creative sequels is a wish to do Disney-like work featuring "The Peer Gynt Suite." There is also a wish to do the classic storytelling of works such as *Babar* and *My Secret Garden*. A second theme centers on the imaginative. As one producer said, his ideal is "full-blown fantasy and entertainment." Producers would like to take animation to the limits of both its potential and their imagination. Associated with the imaginative is a third theme—diversity. Producers envision a variety, including shows based on books, drama, classics, and deductive reasoning. Within that diversity, they also envision better animation cartoon humor, slapstick humor, and suspenseful action/adventure. Some wish for the ghost story, and the suspenseful cliff-hanger. Their countenance drops as they point out that they cannot currently have cliff-hangers. To many that is the core of really classic storytelling. In a fourth theme, producers look toward strong character relationship-type programming (for example, current sequel to the 1955 classic "Rin Tin Tin"). Children themselves could be invited to do some of the imaginative programming—films, animations, and so forth. There would be a combination of classic sequels and imaginative humor, breadth, and diversity.

It is interesting to hear producers acknowledge that they would not want total absence of constraints. As one producer said, "It's hard to imagine no constraints and I'm not sure I believe in that. We get very self-indulgent." Short of no constraints, they would like the opportunities to ply their wistfulness and bring it to children's programming.

Ideal Approximations in Existing Programming

As producers recall their program involvements, they can name shows that have come close to their concept of the ideal. Filmation Studio executives feel a strong sense of pride and accomplishment in "Fat Albert." Its model and its ability to speak solidly and meaningfully to blacks as well as to their multi-ethnic peers is seen as groundbreaking and highly significant. Strong, clearly defined characters and relationships are remembered. Many see those characteristics within the "Smurfs." They admire and respect the warmth in relationships, and they believe that children find in Papa Smurf the ideal dad—warm, caring, with a strong belief in justice.

Producers are aware of how critical it is to keep up the integrity of the history behind characters, and those associated with the program make continuous efforts to assure that integrity. Within that assurance and clear character delineation, viewers can experience surprise when a given character acts differently. That prompts the child to think and be concerned about a character. "Scooby Doo's" strong personality and nonviolent action/adventure gain prominent acknowledgment. "Mickey Mouse Club" and "The Flintstones" also are considered classic examples of programming with a few very clearly defined characters. Imaginative comedy, such as a teletype utilizing woodpeckers and the animal-in-garbage-can garbage disposal, are seen as both progressive and creative for the time in which they were written. "Land of the Lost" is recognized for its strong relationships and fantasy, and "Gatey Hopkins," for its classic story strength and depth.

Formula-Type Theme

If there is a winning formula in children's programming, it lies in the realms of comedy and strong characters.

> Traditionally comedy holds up longer, has had more longevity than anything else. "Scooby Doo," "Jetsons," "Flintstones," and so forth. People follow characters more than action. Action/adventure contains a lot of science fiction-type, [and] becomes outdated.

> Good solid stories are always valuable. People watch people. If they like the characters they'll watch the show.

In variations on this theme it is suggested that first-class entertainment and full-blown fantasy will be a success. But the "if" may be larger than the reality of formula success. In the words of one well-known producer:

I'd like to say yes (there is a formula), but not really. You can have two shows with three people and a dog. One will be a success, one a failure. It's the magic, the chemistry, and how it's developed.

The most thought-provoking perspective on formula is the suggestion that "Formula is what everybody's doing." In this context, it is strongly felt that producers need to break out of the formula cycle if there is any hope for the truly original. This hope lies deeply embedded in the freedom issue as producers perceive it.

Freedom Issue

For most of us, freedom is an elusive concept in the best of times, and it is a particularly troublesome one for producers. If you were to ask them whether networks tell producers how to produce, directors how to direct, and writers how to write, their immediate response would be "Yes, it's true." We have seen examples of the sometimes poor treatment of children's programming legends by new children's programming executives. Also troublesome is the networks' leverage over who does the writing, the voices, and the directing. Producers consider the degree of network involvement to be more extensive in the area of children's programming than in prime time. One producer with extensive experience in both areas characterized the difference this way:

> The difference between experience with "The Virginian" at Universal Studios and in children's television the last nine years. Where there was tremendous latitude on the former with no network interference, it was just the opposite in children's programming. Networks are very, very strong here . . . very, very much involved in the script and flex their muscles a great deal. Sometimes you're topically constrained. For example, homosexual and gun control stories. They also didn't want to do one about death or about a fake minister.

Network leverage over writing and direction is seen in a variety of ways by producers:

> It is a necessary evil . . . a tug of war between their superimposing their ideas regarding what they want . . . great difficulty, but they're not show people. They're rewriting scripts, pulling strings . . . have to have their OK on who the writer will be and who the director will be. Any list that excludes others is a terrible thing and I think it's awful when someone who doesn't know is making up that list.

> The networks are dabblers. Allowing them to choose the writers, pick the voices, . . . I don't see any end. We give them more to get a buy.

The following perspective is from a former network executive who sees both sides of the issue:

> We are told—certainly to an extent they can tell us what they want. They're the client . . . they're the broadcaster. It's like the shoe store trying to talk you into black shoes when you want brown ones. They are as restrictive as you allow them to be, and if you allow them they will tell you word-for-word how to write a script. The reason is they haven't gotten what they wanted and they're very frustrated. If you don't get what you want you tend to do it yourself or tell people what to give you. Probably the biggest wedge that exists between networks and producers today is that issue. I feel a personal as well as professional responsibility to do something about diminishing that wedge.

Some producers believe they could partially stem the control tide, but they admit they are notably hampered in any efforts to do so. They must appeal to a closed shop-type atmosphere of three network clients and, in seeking to please, they make concessions and deals that work against any sense of esprit de corps among themselves. It is tough for competitors to work together in bringing change, especially when that change could affect their own livelihood within a very narrow client market.

Within this dilemma, any change or resolution of conflict seems difficult to implement. There are hopes for change, and some individuals feel a very strong, personal commitment to that end.

> It's gotten so divisive. What I care about is making good shows that are successful.

Seeing a chance for transforming destructive aspects of the producer/network atmosphere into more productive ones, this producer is deeply committed to that goal.

Beyond the individual commitment to change, there is no single mind among producers as to how change can come about and who will initiate it. Some producers believe they can initiate change through the ideas they submit to the networks. Others believe the networks have to initiate change through their buys, and the nature and quality of the purchased programming. A third group of producers believes the process of change can happen only in a context of cooperation and collaboration built around close, professional-level interaction—as distinct from supplier-level interaction—between producers and network executives.

8
The Network Children's Programming Executive

*C*hildren's programming executive does not conjure the flood of images and associations we likely would make to the term *producer.* Gone now are the mirror glasses, the deep tan, the director's chair, and the expensive casual outfit. In their place, we find our image of the corporate executive office—large, paneled, plush, with a panoramic view of downtown Los Angeles or, perhaps, the Pacific. As the image translates into reality, the office size notably diminishes and pine paneling fades—along with the view of downtown or the Pacific. The office space is adequate, simple, and efficient. The view is maybe a shopping plaza, but more likely a studio roof or Johnny Carson's infamous downtown Burbank. It is a practical world of business, scripts, ratings, and schedules.

Profile and Career Paths

Executives in network children's programming are more homogeneous than the production community. They range in age from barely thirty to forty-five, with distinct clustering in the early and mid-thirties. Executives are a younger group than producers and have fewer years experience in the industry and little production background. Whereas nine years of experience would constitute a relative newcomer to production, it would be a veritable "old timer" in the children's programming executive ranks.

Profiling the median of this group would be an executive who is thirty-five years old and has been in children's television programming for three years. The executive is virtually assured to be "she," and "she" is likely to have the B.A. degree. Her major may have been child development, elementary education, or communications, slightly leaning toward the latter, although the former are not unusual. She may or may not have had course background in child development. Those with communications backgrounds are unlikely to have had child development courses, whereas those in elementary education have significant course depth in this area. Those who have had this course background find it a definite help in their work. Those without this course background consider it unimportant, and in one notable instance, a detriment.

Found within this diverse range of individual backgrounds is a tremendous testimony to individual initiative and perseverance in the face of formidable odds. For example, a divorced woman with two children has no source of support. She gets a radio station job, and successfully juggles all the pressures and responsibilities of having a career and being a divorced parent. With only a high school degree, she works her way up to an executive position with a major network. Her path is not the typical one, but her ability and drive have achieved industrywide recognition. And her ambitions are beyond her present post.

A second case also begins with a divorced female parent. She aspires to be a teacher, working as a network secretary during the day and going to school at night. After much persistence, she receives the M.A. degree in child development. Her stamina has already proven her equal to the most formidable executive challenge, and she brings both competence and child sensitivity to her executive position.

A third case, probably the most common, begins with the B.A. degree. Work in the television industry is not a preconceived goal but becomes a natural extension. She begins as a secretary at a production company, advances to assistant to the producer, and then moves to a network. While working with a network film series, the entry-level management position opens and she applies. This woman is unique in that her path included production prior to coming to the network.

In a final case, the woman has taught elementary school and is amazed at the influence of television on children. She subsequently works with a regional television network affiliate and advances to network executive status. Within her background is teacher sensitivity to the nature of the television influence on children.

Importance of Child Development Background

As already discussed, the perceived importance of a child development background varies depending on the individual's own background. For the most part, children's programming executives consider the child development background important and valuable. The following are supportive comments:

> Definitely! You have to be aware of what children can understand at what ages. There are differences in the hunor they and grown-ups understand. Satire, for instance, they don't understand till they are nine or ten.

> I think it is important. I find it a real important part of my background . . . understanding children and really focusing and caring about the kids, staying in

tune to the audience, their likes and dislikes, fads, understanding their phases of development and how they watch television, and the logic of what goes on in a typical household on Saturday morning.

A mid-range perspective will carry these tones:

> I was helped by it but it's not absolutely necessary. A lot of it is more common sense—thinking like a child . . . our target audience being six to eleven. In that sense I was always preparing myself for this job, not knowing this would be the job I was ultimately going to have.

This spectrum is completed with the comment from one network executive that child development courses are "not important . . . a detriment . . . wouldn't be helpful."

Someone now considering a network executive career in children's programming would find a college background and familiarity with child development helpful. The Horatio Alger roads are still open to the bright and the determined, but competition in the executive marketplace has escalated. Even reluctant producers now admit that child development courses are helpful to the network executive.

Basic Criteria in Program Idea Evaluation

When a program idea comes to the network, what are the basic issues the network executive will have in mind as the evaluation begins? There are several, and among them are some prominent, common threads. Strong, well-defined characters are sought. The beloved among children's programming over the years has had characters with personality strength. In the words of one executive:

> It's really gut instinct, and the gut instinct is supported by personality and characters . . . whether the characters make you laugh or smile. Comedy has a stronger intrinsic value than action/adventure. I like action/adventure for later in the morning . . . for the older kids. The typical situation of what goes on in the home is the younger kids get up early and the "hot levels" are lower, so you program younger shows. As more and more kids get up the concept of the shows gets a little bit older until in the afternoon you try to incorporate teens and young adults—especially young males—into your audience. It doesn't mean the younger kids aren't watching. It just means the audience has a larger percentage of older children and adults.

In addition to strong characters, the concept of fun is important. As one executive said, "I want the kids sitting there eating their Froot Loops or whatever to laugh . . . to get into the show." A third criterion is longevity. The executives are aware that fads last for six months or so and then fade. To come in on the trailing edge of a fad (for example, break dancing) could be disastrous. One executive spends considerable time traveling and "milieu experiencing" for the primary purpose of "sniffing the children's orientations" and the trends that have not yet dawned as fads. It is a difficult task to predict where children will be a year from now and to program evaluate that far in advance. Obviously the media could produce the fad in some instances, but it is better to know enough about the trend horizon to join the flow at the point when it is becoming more rapid.

The first-ranking network from the previous season has the least choice among program ideas from the production houses. Understandably, network executives are pleased with the general performance of their schedule during the previous season, and they are not likely to make drastic changes. Production houses, knowing well their market for sales, will save their finest ideas for the markets where they anticipate considerable buying potential. In this instance, we are referring to the second- and third-ranking networks, hungry to improve their ratings. One point in market shares can make a considerable difference in advertising revenues, and networks are eager to improve their competitive position. In one sense, the first-ranking network is at a severe disadvantage, seeing little of the new program array that will be seen by its competitors.

In another sense, the network executives are aware that the selection is limited. This limiting process stems from the production house tendency to pitch an idea to a network individual. When an idea is taken to one network, it may be pitched quite differently from the version taken to another network. One executive who regularly experiences this aspect of production house marketing described it this way:

> What I don't like is ABC Children's Programming is Squire, NBC Children's Programming is Phyllis, CBS Children's Programming is Judy, and they pitch to each differently. They know what pushes Judy's button, they know what pushes Phyllis's button, they know what pushes Squire's button, and so forth.

As one executive characterized it, "It's a very astute game. Everybody knows."

Evaluation Independence

Once a program idea captures the fancy of a key children's programming executive, it will be seen by numerous others on its way to ultimate acceptance or rejection. As it begins this network journey, the question is whether children's programming will weigh the idea independently or whether it will be a review and decision-making process engaged in jointly and closely with other departments such as broadcast standards. In each network instance, the children's programming executives report that they review independently within the general context of a close working relationship with broadcast standards and with research. There are variations on this theme, but they tend to preserve in each instance the stated sense of independence:

> We review independently. We have a sane, intelligent group of practices people. They don't deal in absolutes, they deal with the whole. They have been very daring [in specific program instances].

> We work closely with broadcast standards and with the research department. We also have a social science advisory panel from across the country. We find ideas we like but before we make a decision we get input from all those different areas. From research we want to know where kids are today. From broadcast standards we need to relate the program to network standards. And from the social science advisory panel we need to learn the child development aspect, how children will perceive what we're presenting and what the possible dangers are or what the possible benefits are.

> We rely on the judgment and insights of individual consultants and have our advisory panel [individuals here named]. They're down to earth and can tell me on a kids' level, for example, how I can simplify this idea. For example, in the "Smurfs," one of our story editors pitched the idea of a story on death. Our initial response to the idea was negative—as being inappropriate for these young children. We took it to the social science advisory panel and really hashed it out. We still wouldn't have done it, but we were swayed by them. We wanted their input to do it right. Every year we go back to them and say, "Here are some things we're thinking of doing. Should we, and if so how do we go about it? For example, how do we tell a Smurf story that deals with child safety?" Response we got to that one was, "Are you kidding? The Smurfs are always going off with strangers! Put that idea in Mister T. Smurfs is not the place for it." We did just that.

With its social science advisory panel's encouragement and guidance, NBC's "Smurf" program on death received an Emmy.

Consultants are involved to varying degrees in the review process at each of the three networks. Whereas an advisory panel and base-touching with individual panel members is the style at NBC, ABC looks to Bank Street College of Education. CBS functions more on an individual consultant basis. The intensity and frequency of consulting also vary. It is unlikely that consultant input would be the critical factor in whether to purchase a program, but as we have seen, there can be considerable influence on topics and how they are treated within program development.

Ideal Children's Programming

Whether it be live action or cartoon, the family theme is a consistent one among children's programming executives. As one executive said of ideal programming, "I'd have a family situation . . . a group of kids getting along. I like to create family situations that mirror what children are experiencing." Some executives feel that the Bill Cosby show (prime time) is an example of the kind of family programming that approximates the ideal. Family in the animation context is associated with the "Smurfs" as an ideal:

> The characters are all there and they care about each other. It's such a great platform for all sorts of things. It's a community of people who care about each other, but they can argue. Why do you think Papa Smurf is the number one character with kids? Because he is the ideal parent . . . he's the ideal grownup. He's understanding, he punishes when punishment is called for, he explains, he's always there to take responsibility, in a situation of crisis he's there . . . the perfect adult.

The platform this executive refers to is the opportunity to deal topically with the issues and problems common to the experience of families and children. "Kids wanted the show. Before the show we were 23–24 market shares. When this show came on we were 45 shares. Some markets get a 50 share. Some cities get a 55 share."

To "mirror what children are experiencing" takes us a step beyond family setting programming. Non-ABC executives cite the ABC Weekend Specials as ideal, and there is a strong desire for more dramatic types of programs—"not so much programs dealing with social issues but with kids' feelings and with social problems." These dramas could be in areas such as name calling, dealing with fighting parents, and so forth.

There is notable contrast between the wistfulness of programming executives and that of producers. Among executives we do not find thoughts of imaginative sequels to the classics nor do we find the imaginative, full-blown fantasy entertainment. There is not a desire to take animation to its creative limits. We do not hear the word *diversity* being used in reference to programs on books, classics, and deductive reasoning. The one theme producers and programming executives do hold in common is strong character/relationship-type programming. Beyond that common ground, producers are much more centered on the imaginative, the creative, and the exploration of the fantasy limits of the medium.

Ideal Approximations in Existing Programming

From the perspective of the programming executives, their ideals among existing shows are "The Smurfs," ABC Weekend Specials, and prime-time "Bill

Cosby." Ray Bradbury's "The Electric Grandmother" is mentioned as being sensitive to a child's feeling of loss and treats topics creatively and imaginatively. "Monchichis," in its unsuccessful ABC bid to unseat the "Smurfs," gains acknowledgment for its strong characters, good story, and educational values. In one of its shows, for instance, it went against the notion of girls rivaling one another for a male's affection.

Whereas one could generally envision a distinction between the *ideal* and the *actual* in children's programming, that distinction does not exist among programming executives. Their ideals are actual programs. Perhaps the producer/executive contrast reflects relative proximity to budgets and ratings, the executives less able to be creative because they are closer to the realities of the TV industry. Perhaps, too, it reflects a difference in experience and orientation. Many executives have had no experience in production, and their ideal would not be the art/animation background characteristic of many producers. Still a third "perhaps" relates to pride in one's program selections. Whereas the programming executive is in a selection position, the producer is not. The programming executives select and make investment in given program properties. Like an initiation process or a difficult purchase decision, it is natural to increase our liking for that which we have selected.

Formula-Type Themes

There is one formula-type theme that spans eras. Network executives and producers are well aware that comedy is universal.

> You watch a comedy over and over again. Kids will watch the "Scoobies," "Flintstones," "Smurfs," over and over again. Action/adventure things—"Mr. T," "Spiderman," "Thundar"—you get 'em once and you may not get them again.

An element in successful comedy is strong characters. That concept can be applied to any of the comedy forms—straight comedy, comedy-adventure, or comedy action. One executive remembered the experience of first coming into the children's programming executive position:

> "Flash Gordon" was on the air . . . and I thought I had made a career mistake. I thought, "If that show works I'm really in the wrong department, really in the wrong place 'cause if that show works I do not understand why." . . . And Flash Gordon didn't work because it didn't have any characters . . . it didn't have any relationships. They were like plastic people . . . no emotion . . . you didn't know anything about them . . . and it just didn't work. Luckily I was right . . . and I'm still here. The animation on it looked terrific, but it's not enough.

Perception of Producers

Programming executives see producers as creative artists and suppliers. This combination has conflict built into it, and we see different aspects of this conflict within the comments of the executives:

> I see them as the people who should have the overall vision for the project. In some cases they don't get that creatively involved. In other cases they feel they have to do everything. Perception is case-by-case. Sometimes [we're seen as] supportive and helpful, other times as a pain, interfering, a necessary evil. Some ask for our input and support . . . others would just as soon we never see them again.

> Artist. I see them as very creative. I wouldn't ever take that away from them.

> Artists. For Joe Ruby to turn a basic Rubik's Cube into that series and make it work, it takes a great deal of creativity. I have tremendous respect for the producing community, and their having to put up with us. They take input from both standards and programming, put it in, and make it work. That alone is creative talent.

> I see them as all of these [artist, craftsman, servant] . . . and, in addition, suppliers. I was a producer for a number of years and we used to complain about "can't do the show I want to do." Later I became an executive producer and had producers working for me. Then I worked with budget, show, and whatnot, and it was a transformation. They're artists. They're very creative, and they're also very practical. They know what the limits are and they'll always go for as much as they can beyond the limit. And they also protect their writers, which is what they're supposed to do. I think if the producer had his druthers there'd be nobody out there. I bet you'll find that all the way down this hall. . . . Steven Bochco would love to do "Hill Street Blues" his way 100 percent, but he takes some network suggestions. But we're all going through the same thing. We're coming across well. I never tell a producer, "Do it this way!" because then he becomes very defensive.
>
> There was an insightful comment from an executive producer of mine. "Remember, writers are soap bubbles. You got to keep them up. Always got to keep them up. As soon as you get them down here then you're not going to be able to get them up, and they're not going to be able to do it for you." I've always remembered that. They're very sensitive.

Self-Identity/Teacher Role

Most programming executives do not see themselves as teachers. Where there is a glimmer of teaching within their self-identity, it comes in a secondary role.

I find myself reading scripts and looking to see where I might get some information in there . . . something that's kind of a prosocial message. That's not why they [the kids] turn it on. You know, the kids don't come to television to learn, but you hope that what they take away is something positive, and you know they're going to take something away from it.

[I am a teacher] only in a secondary role. I try to entertain kids. There's nothing more wonderful than to hear children laugh. It makes you sad when you've worked this hard and they don't laugh. Our job is to make children laugh. There's nothing more gratifying than to sit with nephews and nieces and have them laugh at all the right times . . . and be scared at the right times.

By comparison, the teacher emphasis, although still moderate, is more evident among programming executives than it is among producers. In the production context, entertainment has a virtually singular goal. Producers are professional entertainers of children, very knowledgeable in their profession, yet they see themselves in sharp contrast to school-related activity in the child's typical week. Although the general tone among executives also is in this vein, some have within their self-direction the latitude to think in prosocial terms and to "own" a teaching-related role.

Freedom Issue

The programming executive role is one of program selection. Executives are the buyers—the clients of producers; they shape the product. This raises the freedom question that Muriel Cantor phrased in 1969, that "networks are telling producers how to produce, directors how to direct, and writers how to write."[1] As programming executives look at their contemporary setting, the freedom issue comes into focus, and the focus depends on the network and the perspective of the individual executive. Some characterize it as "constant interactive conflict," seen as a given of the industry:

There is that constant interactive conflict. We have approval over writers, directors, voices, and casting. Ideally network and producers are partners. I want them to speak their piece. Network pays the freight. If producers don't think network should have that right they should pay for their shows. If they believed in themselves they perhaps would.

Others suggest moderate, suggestion-type intervention.

In some cases at some networks you may find that [network telling] to be extremely true. Here it's more a process of a lot of involvement in the form of suggestions. Some producers are comfortable with suggestions. Mostly it's a kind of give and take and I think the process works faily well. How do they see us? Probably network interference. I really think they see us as people that have suggestions. It depends on the relationship.

It's very true. We don't tell them how to do it but have a lot of input. They see us as getting a little too involved. The relation to the networks can be adversarial, but it's fun to work with them.

The executive/producer relationship may vary depending on the individuals involved, their relationship, their mutual respect and trust:

We certainly do that [laughs]—a case-by-case basis. A lot depends on how much faith you have in the people creating the product. Sometimes you don't know how far to let them go. You always want to work with someone with strong, creative vision. Sometimes you think you're sharing a particular vision and all of a sudden it doesn't seem like you're looking through the same set of glasses.

Others describe a close-knit family—loving, differing, fighting, apologizing, and making up.

[Executives dominating producers] is not true for ABC. Maybe a few years ago, but not true now. [The relationship is] very warm and giving. We fight like family and that's how I like to look at it. We are all family and we fight, make up, apologize, scream at each other, call back and say, "I'm sorry, I didn't mean that." I don't think of us as adversaries.

For some producers, the close-knit aspects of this relationship are likely very real. Others become aware that this same set of dynamics—loving, differing, fighting, apologizing, and making up—characterize the battered spouse syndrome. The question becomes one of degree and distinctions. It is clear that producers find the interactive problems more alarming than do executives, and for some producers the perceived level of conflict has reached crisis-type proportions, each side locked into a syndrome that negates healthy growth for either. There is no evidence of this crisis atmosphere among programming executives. One programming executive, taking a business perspective on the producer/network interaction in the context of freedom, suggests:

If you go to the bank for a loan, you're giving up certain things in terms of freedom. I don't like that producer complaint. If they don't like it, then they should stop using our money. You can't have it both ways.

Reference

1. Muriel Cantor, *The Hollywood TV Producer: His Work and His Audience* (New York: Basic Books, 1971).

9
The Network Broadcast
Standards Executive

Depending on your perspective, the term *broadcast standards* could bring to mind either protectors or villains. For some, their image is that of "the judge," weighing programming elements carefully and methodically, and assuring fairness. For others, the image might be one of the federal inspector, examining carefully the programming structure to assure that it is safe and will not bring future repercussions on the industry. Still others see caring individuals who know how the product is to be consumed by children, and want to be sure that consumption is not harmful, converting it to helpful wherever possible. And yet another group sees the "Grinch that Stole Creativity," the "nay sayers" dead set on blocking any hint of the creative for fear of the dangerous. There could be still other images, but these provide the spectrum and its breadth.

Profile and Career Paths

Like programming executives, those in broadcast standards are more homogeneous than the production community. They range in age from the mid-twenties to the mid-fifties, and their experience in the industry could be as little as one month or as much as twenty-three years. Profiling the median of this group, we would find an executive who is thirty-eight years old and has been in broadcast standards for eight years. The executive is equally likely to be "he" or "she," and is likely to have the M.A. degree. Degree major is most likely to have been child development or child psychology, and the range of majors includes English and experimental psychology. Education range is more diverse than in children's programming or production. That range spans the entire distance between the Harvard Ph.D. and the high school diploma. Course experience in child development is prominent. Those having majored in experimental psychology or nonpsychology areas are unlikely to have had this course experience. Those who have the course background consider it valuable to their broadcast standards work, and those without the background think having the background would not hurt. In the words of one executive, "Child development background is a good way to get the attention of people who feel we should take special trouble to get people qualified in specific areas. It is looked upon favorably." In this area, as well as in programming, there is multi-ethnic representation. By contrast, the producer community is predominantly white males.

Within the backgrounds of the broadcast standards executives, there is a fascinating diversity. Virtually none of these people lived their childhoods dreaming of working in network broadcast standards. They came to their positions either by happenstance, or as a natural extension of communications interest and involvement.

"Bitten" by College Radio

Well, my background . . . was a lot of college radio as an undergraduate which, I think, imprinted me and undoubtedly came from previous sources as well that kind of peaked in there. Then I stayed in school for a number of reasons, not all of which were particularly worthy, in the late 1960s and very early 1970s and took a Ph.D. in psych at Harvard. You may know that psych at Harvard—although the departments very recently fused—at the time was divided into psychology (which was experimental psychology, sensation and perception, learning, and that sort of thing) and then there was the social relations department which was about four disciplines all of which had social as their first word. And I was most definitely in the psych side of that, not the "soc-rel" side. And [I] tended to be more sympathetic to a biological/behavioral method of analysis rather than what presumably you're trained in.

It became clear to me that I didn't want to end up teaching. Coming out of psych grad school of that sort you're either feeding M&Ms to mental patients or you're teaching college—two things which may sound rather different and probably are. So I tried to figure out when was the last time I had any fun to speak of, and it was back in something like radio. So with all the charm and naivete of a twenty-six-year-old just out of graduate school—or almost out of graduate school—having passed my orals I went down to New York and began knocking on a few doors at a few networks. There you can get an awful lot of rejection letters from local stations—especially if you literally just write to them out of the blue. But I did get a few offers from CBS and took the one I felt most comfortable with, which was editor in program practices. I've been in practices for twelve years at one level or another, slowly moving upward . . . or at least they tell me it's upward. So I was in New York for a year and a half or so and then I moved out to LA.

Extension of Child Development Interests

My background was child development. I had a Bachelor of Science from Mills College of Education, and I worked with Head Start in Harlem. And then I went to London and studied at the Hampstead Clinic with Anna Freud, child psychoanalysis. I did some work with Bowlby and Roberts at the Tavistock. Then I did Head Start in Newark, New Jersey, for two years and then went to Harvard and along the line way back in Harlem got very interested in the self-image of children and what happens when you reflect that back to children. They had given us all these cameras in Head Start and, if you know anything about Instamatic cameras, if the picture is that of a black person the light adjustment tends to focus more on the available light than on the face of the black child. You get sort of your basic "raisin in the sun" and that became an ongoing interest . . . what happens when kids see pictures of themselves. And when I was in London studying with Anna Freud I saw a film done by the community called "Warrendale" which was the first documentary done where people moved into a treatment center for emotionally disturbed children and lived there. And I got very intrigued at how, if you have a background within education or with children how you can adapt the film-making process to make it more understandable to the audience in making films about children. I actually made a film at the Hampstead Research Center, came back, and pounded a lot of doors in New York City . . . that's just when Sesame Street was going on the air. But no one really wanted to talk to you . . . a plain teacher . . . either you were a Ph.D. educator or a film maker, and that sense of bridging the gap really hadn't come into its own. And I want to Harvard and did a lot of work in visual studies—worked with Rudolf Hernheim in visual thinking, took animation, took photography, so that I would learn the skills of the film makers so I could talk more succinctly to them. And then [I] took what classes there were in children and television and the following year Aimee [Dorr] came and they started setting up courses in the area of children and television.

Writer-to-Regulator

I came into this department in 1962 at the behest of the fellow who was then running it. At that time I was a short story writer. I was making a living, but short story writers don't make a notorious amount of money. So he offered me the job, and it seemed secure. The pay was very, very low . . . you just couldn't believe it . . . because, at the time, I think broadcast standards was the unwanted stepchild of the industry. We had been told by the federal government, "Either clean up your act or we'll clean it up for you." So the networks formed their own compliance and practices department. Ours at that time was called "Continuity Acceptance" and then at another time it was called "Standards and Practices," and, finally, "Broadcast Standards" separately from "Compliances and Practices" which now handles another area. I lasted for two years, and just by way of history, I'll tell you that at that time there were seven white males running broadcast standards for NBC. We used to sit up on the fourth floor. It was like a little island . . . literally an ivory tower. We would review scripts. We read them and we tried to find that which we considered would in some way offend the FCC or the NAB or our own management. And we sent out very officious memos . . . they were actually unconditional demands because in those days, if they didn't do what we wanted, we just edited. You'd see somebody's lips moving up and down on the tube and you wouldn't hear anything, and you'd know the censor had been at work. It lasted two years for me and it was too restrictive, so I left. . . . Before that I was a theatrical agent. I was partnered with Byron Griffith, who discovered Connie Stevens, so that tells you how long ago it was. So, when I left NBC in 1964 I went to work packaging for a wonderful guy named Dick Irving Highland. He handled some of the best writers and directors in the business. After a couple of years Mr. Highland had a heart attack and didn't make it, so I started writing freelance and I had . . . not a lot of luck, but I did make a fair living writing for television. In 1972 they asked me to come back. At that time, the network was interested in going into long form and the Head of the Standards Department wanted someone with a writing/industry background to work with the producers because the producers would no longer just take "No."

I taught junior high and high school English prior to coming with NBC. I took a B.A. in sociology with a minor in art. My husband's a teacher. I see my current position as a career, and I like my work.

Program Idea Evaluation

Standards executives agree that imitability is likely their primary up-front issue in children's program evaluation. "Imitability" has a double edge. The light side of imitability encompasses the positive messages a child can learn, for instance, moral and prosocial themes. The shadowed side carries the potentially harmful or negative, acts the child might detrimentally emulate in the star character. At given networks, one side of this issue will hold greater prominence than the other. One network, for instance, highlights the shadowed side, taking a basic, defensive posture that centers on violence. Primary concern is to avoid negative reaction from the "watchdog" groups. Network standards executives point out that these groups count incidents of violence, and base their complaints on the numbers.

The executive says that the network perspective differs from the watchdog concentration on numbers, and considers violence in context. Because of this, executives might allow more rough-and-tumble on a Charlie Brown show than they do on anything else. To them, the child potential for imitability is low and, in any case, relatively harmless, even though there may be a high number of incidents within that given program. Comparable risk-taking agents in another context may be major bases for standards concern. Problems arise if a positive character does something negative that a child viewer might emulate. On the question of imitability one executive said, "I would prefer to err on the side of conservatism in review—deleting any negative aspect a child might emulate."

A second up-front issue is role balance. Standards executives consider the roles of women and those of minorities. They have an interest in maintaining both a power role and a representational balance, assuring that minority group members and women get power role castings. They feel, at times, as though the representational balance issue puts them in a no-win situation. In 1972, native Americans protested release of the movie "Ahonte-Yo." More recently, womens' groups protested a movie done on rape because no care was given to the rape victims. Blacks and Hispanics have protested their role depictions, and Pacific Asian Americans have been protesting their seemingly nonexistent status in television series. Gays have protested their media treatment, saying the only time they are portrayed is in joke-type depiction, someone "limpwristing his way across the stage." Each group, in turn, has expressed its concerns. Broadcast standards, wanting to avoid offending its consumers, has listened and, in specific instances, has responded.

A third issue is one described as tone, texture, and morals. Standards executives ideally hope the lead characters in a program will embody constructively positive qualities children can respect and emulate. Beyond the simple "good versus evil" thematic formula, they want the program to have a positive moral tone. They also are keenly aware that specific elements within programs can have terrifying potential for children. In this context, executives frequently live a rather schizophrenic existence because they openly encourage producers to test the limits in areas such as violence. When producers respond to their encouragement, standards executives, in turn, make contextual judgments.

Standards to Context Evolution

Broadcast standards has experienced an evolution over the years, notably changing the complexion of rules and regulations into one of reviewing an element within its context. Standards executives describe the early years of their work as having been too restrictive. "While we thought we were doing a job, what we were really doing was creating a situation wherein there was a fear of going too far, of offending someone. The result of that was that we started dealing in stereotypes . . . the stereotype was the 'quick fix.' " And with the inadvertent series of stereotypes came wide-ranging public complaint. Hearing from individuals always had been a part of standards experience, but the number and intensity was unprecedented, and included large, national groups such as the Parent-Teacher Association (PTA), native Americans, women, blacks, and Hispanics.

The change in standards practices was multifaceted. Whereas the early executive ranks had been exclusively white males, the scene notably evolved to include women, Asians, Hispanics, and blacks. At given networks, this diversity now constitutes a staff of resident experts on standards issues relating to roles, stereotypes, and how a given event might impact a specific ethnic group within the viewing public. In addition to staff changes bringing diversity, the activity itself has changed as well. The early days of the script-reading/negative-memo sequence have become the current scene in which there are no lists of do's or don'ts.

> We're not cluttered with "Gee, we can't do." You know programming always wants to go that step beyond, and we expect them to . . . we expect them to keep pushing because we're finding more and more that the viewers really will accept more . . . so long as it's not tasteless, too graphic, or gratuitous.

The key concepts in standards review today are "gratuitous" and "context." Broadcast standards staff are expected to judge things contextually.

> How does this play? And we have found that if it plays . . . if it's valid or relevant in context, most of the viewers don't mind. They mind when you demean someone or insult them by using material gratuitously.

As you can see, it is almost impossible to separate "gratuitous" from "context." It is context that determines what is or is not gratuitous. A glance at the day-to-day standards process gives us a better understanding of how gratuitous is determined. Gratuitous, in context, asks the question, "Why was that necessary?"

> We had a show where the lead, who was a very handsome fellow, was never with a girl. And there was concern by either our programmers or the supplier that people might think he was not interested in girls. So, the very next episode opened with a phone call. You come in on a marvellously manicured hand reaching over for the phone. The camera follows up the hand and you see the most delightful cleavage you've ever seen—gorgeous girl picks up the phone and says, "Yes?" Then she rolls over and says, "It's for you, sweetheart." He answers the phone and then bang, he's on a case. We never saw the girl again! I thought that was gratuitous.

In the area of sex content, the standards message to producers is a consistent one: "Use your own judgment," and "don't overshoot." Even while delivering the message, standards executives know they have given the producers a personal invitation to overshoot, and that they want producers to test the limits this way:

> They know what they're doing. A lot of times they overshoot, and we'll look at the rough-cut. . . . One of the best pilots I've ever seen . . . was like watching a theatrical. They did an entire scene with a stripper. Now, there were some shots in there . . . woof! . . . but they were just too much for us, so we asked them to trim it after the rough cut. But even there, when we went on paper after our conversation with the producer *before* he shot the scene, we just said simply, "Provide coverage and avoid graphics. Don't have her doing a bump-and-grind into camera." So we get into that [telling producers what to do] but hopefully not in a dictatorial fashion. We don't want them to think

about broadcast standards. We want them to think about bringing the best product they can to us. In the three years I've been sitting in this chair I think we've done four edits . . . four, that's all.

As gratuitous yardsticks extend into the violence area, they weigh heavily on avoiding the graphic and the gruesome:

> We don't want to see someone with his face blown away with a shotgun. . . . So I guess we do get into direction in that respect, but we leave it up to the producers' good judgment. . . . In other words, we're saying to the producer, "Have your director get a lot of shots on that particular scene so that if there is one area we consider a little bit too brutal, we can go to a reaction shot" [on an onlooker].

Do standards executives within this process "tell producers how to produce, directors how to direct, and writers how to write"?

> I think it's very true of [our] network. I think there's no question about it. I think that's clearly something that has been labeled rightly in our program review process. I think it's getting more so.

> That sounds like the standard comment from the producers out there who are saying, "We're clearly the experts. What are these self-appointed creative types who can't even get a decent job making programs . . . what are they doing over there at the network nitpicking these shows to death?" That is certainly a common complaint which is by no means confined to the children's area. . . . The scripts, storyboards, every element . . . the extent to which we influence these elements . . . we don't go around telling people what would be more effective in terms of creative results. We're fairly sensitive about avoiding that. We don't feel it's any of our business and we feel it might exacerbate a relationship which is sometimes threatened by other things that we tell people they can't do. But if we're afraid that a director is going to direct something in a way that's going to exaggerate emotional content or certain frightening content or certain antisocial potential or that something is being written in such a way or someone has put in a racial slur without even being aware of it, or something that takes for granted a certain sex role that we feel uncomfortable with or any of those things . . . sure, we'll tell them what not to write and we may suggest how they could write it in a way . . . we'll give them examples of what would work. We won't say, "This is what you must change it to." We'll say, "Please don't do this, and among the things you might do that we would find acceptable would be something like this or this or this."

> Yeah, sure, we're telling everybody how to do everything when we feel that what they've proposed to us is something we don't want to see on the screen. So I can be quite snotty about it in that respect.

I don't want anyone in our department to play programmer and begin producing and, by the same token, I don't want the producer to self-censor. We want to avoid that direction. We will ask them to avoid the gruesome, the grotesque . . . [it's] direction in that respect.

They see us restricting their freedom and to some extent we do. We see ourselves as buyers who have a right to input regarding the nature of the product we're buying.

Producer/Standards Executive Relationship

The nature of the producer and standards executive relationship is, by its very structure and definition, predestined to be an adversarial one. As the industry's "nay-sayers," standards executives naturally consider themselves ripe for caricature and negative feelings from producers.

They hate us. They see us saying "No, no, no." Generally they're nice around us, though.

The conflicts aren't the most pleasant. The feeling you get is the classic position of being the bad guys. We don't just say no to things. We change things, ultimately to get it on the air rather than to keep it off. It seems to me that being a producer would be better than doing this.

Producers see [me] very negatively. I personally have the toughest reputation. I come in with a child development background. . . .

Roles

Within that conflict-ridden setting producers have very distinct and diverse conceptions of their own roles ranging from judge and jury to quality control and the protectors of children. It is evident that the perceived roles are as diverse as the individual executives themselves and the different industry settings in which they function.

Judge and Jury

There are elements of enforcement. I would hesitate to say police because of the connotations. Judge and jury leaps to mind because although there are methods of appeal, we're pretty powerful.

Company Protector

We're protecting the company from the potential excesses of the suppliers and even our own programming people.

Caring Parent

> I ask, "If a child looks at this, what are they going to take away? Should my 4 1/2 year old see this? What will she take away from it? What should we be saying to them?"

Frustrations within Standards Role

Being the resident rule maker carries with it feelings of frustration, and many standards executives wish for the chance to make the plays rather than to call them. There is little attention or reward for positive achievement. The fan response latitude is destined to be far greater on the negative end than on the positive end. Occasionally the standards executive hears a producer say, "You've forced us not to take the easy way. Thanks. We think it's a better scene." And when the comment comes, the executive stands in disbelief.

As one standards executive said, "I'm frustrated with having to be the 'no sayer' that producers hate. I hope the changes recommended have made a difference for some viewer." The executives often will never know the ultimate effect of, for instance, having a lead character fasten his or her seat belt, but they nurture the hope that they have made a difference.

Perceptions of Producers

As producers extend their "network radar," they feel they are seen in the role of servant/supplier. Network executives place a notably different perspective on that picture.

> I see them drawing together talent which is trying to go a lot of different directions and harnessing it to serve a vision which they in the end must have. I can't think of anything harder to do.

> I see them as professionals.

> It's important to respect producers—stimulate dialogue and trust. That's tough because [our network] is dictatorial. It should be their show and craft, but that's not true. It's not the way it works. The more cooperation, the more you get back.

Standards executives are well aware that they are dealing with artists and professionals. They are equally aware that they are dealing with strong egos. They respect both and know that the realities of their setting are destined to come across as respecting neither.

Independence Issue

Within each of the three networks, the standards department functions independently. At NBC, the vice-president of Broadcast Standards reports directly to the head of the legal division's broadcast group level in New York.
This is the same reporting path followed by the programming department. There
is no point at which the standards department would be intimidated or diluted
by a reporting structure that channeled it through programming, marketing,
or some other division of the corporation. Comparable reporting structures
are evident at ABC and CBS. CBS standards describes its reporting structure:

> Program practices is not a division. It reports directly to Broadcast Group.
> Therefore we're close to policy considerations. That means we're concerned
> with scheduling as a whole. Is there enough we can point to with pride? There's
> a lot in the middle, and the flaw in the process perhaps is that middle. Our
> job is to make sure what gets on is getting the most brownie points, and there's
> a time problem. The problem is not having enough time. To the contrary,
> sometimes we're not challenged enough because of time.

Here we see a different dimension of the standards picture—standards as a
facilitator of corporate image.

At the more immediate level, standards executives are likely to feel greater
programming pressures in their specific program decision-making process.

> In a meeting there were six people trying to beat me down on issues on a show
> for three hours. It would be easy to give in. The system is there but you have
> to be darn committed.

The review process to which this commitment refers is an extensive one.
Standards executives become involved from the very outset—the premise stage.
They then continue to see every aspect of the program's development as it moves
from premise to outline, outline to script, and then on to storyboards, rough
cuts, and the final program. The rough-cut to final-program stage can prove
the most frustrating. Although executives have had significant input prior to
this stage, recommendations may not have been incorporated to the extent or
in the manner anticipated.

To some, the future of broadcast standards for children looks as uncertain
as its past:

> I think unless our society changes very drastically over the next period of time
> . . . unless we get an administration in the next ten years that cares more about
> regulation for children and television it's going to be an era that people look
> back on. I mean it's fast becoming that.

10

The Originality/Creativity Dilemma and Program Buys

Current Program Buys

Commercial television has often been called a "copy cat" medium. When a given type of program works, the networks will do more of it the next season. No one knows this better than Dr. George Gerbner. Having studied the violence patterns in commercial network programming every year since 1969, he observed that program violence increased in the season following the Nielsen ratings success of violent programs.[1] So where there might be one or two shows in a given thematic format one season, the look-alikes may mushroom to a dozen the following season. Frequently writers complain about doing look-alikes rather than being creative in a new direction with a different format.

Sometimes products that have not yet been on the air are copied. They are termed "presold." The network or a production house buys a property and the exclusive right to develop that property into a commercial program for children. It could be a successful children's book and its characters, the star of a movie, or a prime-time show host. In each instance, the principle is the same—a property is bought and developed for commercial children's television.

Creative Process and Presold

The dynamics of "presold" pose a number of hurdles for the creative process. The first hurdle is presold itself. It means the producer has this mass of "already-defined" sitting in the middle of the drawing board. It is a major, defined given that must be fit into whatever scenes and settings are developed. And they, by virtue of the presold property, are likely to be largely developed, too. Contrast this picture with the other end of the spectrum—the formation of Children's Televison Workshop (CTW). With wide-ranging creative freedom, CTW had $8 million and two years lead time before any program needed to be on the air. Where the predefined is quite large and perhaps all-permeating within presold, the creative field for characters, relationships, and general program approach is wide open with the CTW model. It is the difference between a large, irregular-shaped weight in the middle of a drawing board, and a clean, blank tablet ready for new ideas.

Admittedly, the CTW beginning was a one-time occurrence, but the imaginative within any producer naturally migrates toward this end of the spectrum. Ironically, even network executives admit that the programming with greatest longevity on commercial children's television is that which features original characters and strong relationships. The mood of the presold moment has an appearance of security, but it may well be a short-lived moment.

A second hurdle for the creative process within the presold milieu relates to the time realities in program development. Presold properties frequently are those "hot deals" consummated at the very last minute. They have not gone through the pilot development process of bible, storyboard, and so forth. Instead, they have been the last-minute, nose-out for program ideas which did go through the painstaking process. Therefore, they are surface and, in a basic sense, undeveloped—pushed through the April through August production-crunch process with minimal thought given to the series concept and its development. The milieu is hand-to-mouth and the goal is to get something on the table in time for the new fall season.

A third hurdle is the time in a presold's life when it becomes available for children's program development. When the property is experiencing its prime in its original setting, there is little likelihood that it will become available for children's television programming. With the possible exception of toys, the prime of its original life and context could be negatively affected by its program development for children's televison. Therefore, the property becomes available after it has peaked and is waning. The producer is then faced with trying to revive and successfully market something that has run much of its course in public popularity.

Thus, creativity in the absolute sense is usually not an option for the producer. The framework and its givens are there, frequently shadowing much of the program landscape. To many producers, this kind of setting eclipses their creative energies and imagination. A notable minority of producers find this challenging. As a producer once commented, the network may give you an ash tray and tell you to "make something of it."

> The challenge is to slip in—within those marketing parameters—whatever creative information you can so you don't go home at night and become an alcoholic. In that respect we are allowed to practice our craft . . . a character, a situation, a landscape, or something. The networks don't care what the background looks like.

> There's opportunity to be creative in the design of the show, the look, the direction, the voice work.

They see us as the idea initiators. I don't have any trouble with them. I generally get what I want. It's a very individual thing—depends on the producer and the network.

The analogy is publishing and the print shop. We're almost in the position of the print shop. They [the networks] want it their way. Bit-by-bit we're waiting to be told what to do.

I think we have a lot of room to be creative if we find creative ways to find that room. . . . It's not a given. We are told—certainly to an extent they can tell us what they want.

Presold programming can become one of the most dictatorial tellers to the producer. Working around the edges to be creative in this corner or by that window constitutes an ongoing producer challenge. For some this creativity challenge of the presold era is linked very closely to industry deregulation. This perspective suggests a cause and effect:

When the National Association of Broadcasters dropped its code, the Federal Communications Commission didn't say, "You can't do that!" You didn't find the Strawberry Shortcakes or the GI Joes or the He Man Masters of the Universe on TV prior to 1980, prior to the Reagan administration coming to office and starting to deregulate everything. If the [current] administration or the FCC said, "I think the NAB Code ought to be established again!" you would suddenly find the networks scrambling back to the animation companies for original ideas because they wouldn't be able to use toy lines. Notice that they don't use book lines. They're more difficult to develop, and you have to worry about underintellectualizing them.

In this producer-expressed scenario, deregulation has forced the creative ground to lie fallow while producers are left to wash off the shipped-in vegetables and fruit, making them attractive for resale. Neither producer nor farmer finds this kind of activity indigenous to their creative instincts.

From the creativity perspective, broadcast standards present a double-edged sword. Reinstituting and endorsing the National Association of Broadcasters (NAB) Code might well send broadcasters away from a presold emphasis and more toward original characters and programs. Producers would hail this event as a victory for creativity. It might also have the ripple effect of greater standards consciousness at the networks, and this in turn could prompt producers to self-censor. Standards executives at the networks see self-censorship as the most prominent blow producer creativity can experience. As they formulate and focus a standards emphasis, they see themselves as participating in this creativity demise. In the network perspective, standards and creativity are incompatible.

Do rules institute a rigidity that kills the creative spirit? Much depends on the flexibility built into the rules and their translation in practice. One is reminded of Moreno's thoughts on creativity and the creative process. He acknowledged that the first step in a creative process is to learn the rules exeedingly well. Once this learning process has occurred, the individual then is prepared to break the rules creatively. The primary difference between Moreno's rules and those of television programming is that Moreno refers to the rules of the art or craft itself. Standards-type rules are external to the art or craft. Whether creative peace can be made with these external rules is a difficult question.

Producers and the Ruleless Environment

Erich Fromm once said that we live in existential dilemmas—we want to be governed and yet we hate governmental restrictions.[2] Producers fall within this dilemma. They are not eager to invoke a ruleless environment for their programming. They seem to need and want some degree of clarity and structure. At the same time, they want the freedom to create strong characters and to integrate them into strong, effective storytelling.

> It's hard to write with inspiration when someone is policing and second-guessing. It's also hard to imagine no constraints, and I'm not sure I believe in that. We get very self-indulgent.

Perspectives on Creativity

Glucksberg defined creativity as that capacity for flexibility and spontaneity that enables one to move beyond existing boundaries and assumptions.[3] Haimowitz and Haimowitz termed it the ability to be spontaneously marginal in one's environment, unbound by the rigid and the commonly accepted.[4] For the academic community and the television community alike, identifying creativity has always been easier than defining it. Borrowing Justice Potter Stewart's famous phrase from another context, "I know it when I see it."[5]

The television community and the public have known and honored some of the most striking examples of commercial program creativity. The pioneering creative genius of Hanna-Barbera has given the world a cast of characters to be loved for generations. In Joe Barbera's words:

> [We] had to adapt from a nondialogue medium, which was the "Tom and Jerry" cartoons, to total dialogue on television. All the characters talked! And we ran into some wonderful people who could do as many as nine voices at one recording session if need be. So they switched from voice to voice and they were brilliant. . . . So we had to adapt to survive. It was purely a matter of eating. There wasn't any money at the beginning there at all, but we were fortunate in one degree that we began developing characters which had personality and which

are running today. We still are out there. "Yogi" is still going. "Flintstones" are still going. The "Jetsons" we are just now doing forty more of them and a live feature. We are now going to have a meeting on doing a live "Flintstone" feature. So I sincerely wish that we would get back to developing original characters with longevity and personality, which is not really around at this time. . . . It's easier for me to say I'm going to do "Mr T" as a cartoon than to say I have [an original] cartoon, because they just have no confidence in it, even though the success of the industry was built on original characters. It's got to go back to that.

Freedom and Creativity

Producer Perspective. Each aspect of the production and television community has its own perspective on the creative process and the role of freedom within it. Producers wish for an environment in which their freedom extends from the initial program idea to the development of characters and script. In a setting where they have the freedom to develop original characters and programming, they consider it essential to have the opportunity for maintaining the integrity of those characters in the final network product.

To feel that an original creation has been dramatically changed from its basic character and intent deals a blow to producer creativity and summons the prevalent supplier image. The creativity context preferred among producers would begin with a network signal that original programming was being sought. Producers would then have the maneuvering room and challenge to develop original ideas. Once bought at the development level, the producers then would want the creative freedom to further develop characters and relationships within the original concept. They would see the scope of their professionalism including the selection of director, the development of bible (its characters and relationships), and the selection of voices. Producers want the privilege and the professional respect that will enable them to maintain the originality and the integrity of their creation.

Network Executive Perspective. Network executives at one level consider it their divine right of economics to be heavily involved in the shaping of the product. The issue is one of custom building to meet specifications. As the buyers with potentially substantial investments, network executives consider it their right to make rather detailed specifications, expecting the producer to meet them in order to get a buy. They further expect either to select or to specify the list from which the director will be selected, make the decisions regarding voices, and so forth. From the producer perspective, these network expectations take executives far across the line that compromises creativity and professionalism.

Network executives view themselves as being attuned to the marketplace. They consider themselves current and knowledgeable on the types and the tone of programming that will attract child viewers. It is in this context that they pass judgment on the program and set out to shape its characters, relationships, and general tone. Part of this shaping might include instances like telling Joe Barbera that a given gag approach will not work. The executives consider themselves experts on current humor trends, and they will flex this expertise in the face of the industry's most creative producers. They see themselves as improving the product and making it marketable.

Implications for Creativity and Change

Producers and network executives approach creativity in programming from vastly divergent perspectives. The executive ear is to the market—what will catch child attention early and gain program ratings. This orientation tends to be geared toward more of what has worked in the current market—the familiar "copy cat" or "coattails" syndrome. In this frame of reference, marketability and sales top the list. Creativity is far down in the rankings, well out of priority range. Producers are left with being creative in a scene or in a background.

The producers are much more attuned to innovation, originality, and creativity at the basic programming level. For them, the creative instinct breathes and lives at the program concept level. In their view, a creative, original program will become a popular child discovery in the marketplace, and will gain success as well as longevity.

The markets and market approaches needed to sustain a producer view of creative programming are vastly different from those required by the network view. The producer's original program concept relies on a program running-time in the new season that is long enough to enable children to discover it and to become regular viewers. Network programming executives want immediate results, and will make December decisions on the new fall season that will short-circuit the chances of an original program gaining popularity.

December decisions spell death for original programs. Children begin the fall season viewing year by tuning in the top network. This pattern will continue through the first two months with channel switch-overs coming to light in the third month. Original programming begins to gain its strength within these channel switch-overs, and the remainder of the year constitutes the viewer-building process. A program whose original characters capture the imagination of child viewers continue to do so in a subsequent season or two. This kind of program continuity is beneficial to the network economically, saving the rash of new investments directed toward the immediate results in existing schedules. However, a network programming executive does not have a several-year contract and the chance to build a program schedule. The executive has to monitor the ratings continually and plug the holes in order to retain employment. The cycle is countercreative.

In this cycle, producers outlast children's programming executives. Well-established producers in the children's television programming milieu will last indefinitely, whereas programming executives' days at the network are usually numbered. Translate this disparity into program ideas and you begin to discover another phenomenon that weighs against creativity. Suppose that Producer A approaches Executive A with a given children's program idea. Executive A rejects it. Producer A shelves it for later reference. A few years later, Executive A no longer holds the network post. Producer A heads for the shelf, dusts off the idea, and takes it to the new executive. If rejected, it can be shelved and recycled indefinitely. The idea itself does not change.

Breaking Countercreative Cycles

Ken Mason, President of Quaker Oats, once looked at the Saturday morning programming scene and commented:

> We do not believe any reasonable person can view a typical 8 A.M. to 12 noon Saturday morning period on any of the major television networks and fail to recognize the need for fundamental change in the way our society is using its most powerful and pervasive medium of communication to entertain and enlighten the very young.[6]

His suggestion was to have each network take responsibility for one hour of quality children's programming on Saturday morning. The plan was to simulcast that quality hour on each of the three networks, producing, in effect, a three-hour children's programming block of top quality. His idea quickly encountered major obstacles, primarily because of its implications for competition during that three-hour time period. Nevertheless, it dramatically expressed a concern for the creativity of children's Saturday morning programming.

Ken Mason's idea was one of those rare industry initiatives. Is it possible that initiative from another quarter could successfully turn the creativity tide? How could one negotiate a closer match between the wealth of creative ideas producers have about ideal programming and the narrow range of the marketable among network executives? One producer suggested that the production community could break the countercreative cycle by taking to the networks only innovative and creative new programming. This would force networks to buy somewhere within that creative milieu. But the realism of the situation would weigh against this possibility in much the same way as it did with Mason's suggestion. Producers could be entering into a pact which would abridge the competitive market. As a group they could agree not to buy into and cater to the "copy cat" marketplace. En masse their program proposals to the networks would be creative. However, this concept would soon be destroyed by someone breaking stride with the en masse program proposal block and trying to appeal to the networks.

Executives complain that the same producers bring the same basic ideas time after time. The character names may be changed, but the ideas remain basically the same. They see it as a kind of closed system with no fresh air coming in and the idea pool stagnating. Producers would not agree with that assessment, and when left to their own imagining about ideal children's programming, producers far surpass network executives in creative/innovative thought.

Several production house heads have a strong commitment to creative thought. Margaret Loesch at Marvel Productions, for example, went beyond bringing in new writers to bringing in strictly idea people. She encourages them to create fresh ideas. They may be stories, characters, even treatments of old stories in a refreshing way. This kind of approach she sees as a hope for a creative Saturday morning future. Hanna-Barbera has evening sessions with gifted young writers, familiarizing them with the field and helping them shape their talent. In each instance, the focus is on youth, the bright, the fresh, and the future.

It is possible to have networks take the innovative lead. If a network was successful in this venture, the "copy cats" might work in favor of the creative. Networks have been reluctant to take that kind of creative risk. The Nielsen ratings and their economics tie them closely to the cycle of what has been working. Perhaps more realistic would be a joint effort, consciously made by producers and networks together. Many producers favor that kind of joint effort, and would be willing to participate in it. A vital first step in that kind of effort would seem to be consciousness raising within a relaxed atmosphere of mutual acceptance, perhaps network executives and producers in a retreat-type setting expressing openly the pain of their current situation, how it works to their mutual detriment, and how the beginning of exploration could move them beyond the frenetic in their existing production schedule environment toward the creatively satisfying and innovative.

The combination of consumer groups and federal agencies bringing pressure to bear on producers and networks could improve creativity. The decade beginning in 1970 was an excellent example of this type of joint force pressure. It also gave evidence of how fleeting that pressure can be in the wake of presidential administration changes and corresponding changes in atmosphere. But for a little while, the winds of change were brought to bear on the networks and their advertisers. At times in Federal Trade Commission (FTC) hearings, there was much controversy, but the economics of an industry and the strength of its lobbies prevailed.

References

1. George Gerbner, Larry Gross, Nancy Signorielli, M. Morgan, and M. Jackson-Beeck, "The Demonstration of Power: Violence Profile No. 10," *Journal of Communication* 29(3) (Summer 1979): 177–196.

2. Erich Fromm, *Escape from Freedom* (New York: Avon, 1969), pp. 19–20.

3. Sam Glucksberg, "The Influence of Strength of Drive on Functional Fixedness and Perceptual Recognition," *Journal of Experimental Psychology* 63 (1962): 36–41.

4. Natalie R. Haimowitz and Morris L. Haimowitz, "What Makes Them Creative?," in Natalie R. Haimowitz and Morris L. Haimowitz, *Human Development* (New York: Thomas Y. Crowell Company, 1960), pp. 44–55.

5. Michael S. Bassis, Richard J. Gelles, and Ann Levine, *Social Problems* (New York: Harcourt Brace Jovanovich, 1982), p. 514.

6. *FTC Staff Report On Television Advertising To Children* (Washington, D.C.: Federal Trade Commission, February 1978), p. 202.

Part III
Reflections and Perspectives

11
Conclusions

How does one keep profitability respectable while keeping respectability profitable? Commercial television, by its very definition, has struggled with this challenge from its early beginnings. Even in the eras when respectability was coming under its most heated and severe attacks, viewers were watching in unprecedented numbers. There could be public outrage on the one hand, but the other hand was never far from the TV channel selector. In a way, whether commercial television was respectable seemed almost secondary. It was watched, and as it was watched, it was all the more profitable.

The profit-making role expectation carries its own set of identity problems. What shall I be? What I want to be? Or what other people want me to be? A classic conflict experienced at some level by all of us, and television was no exception. In its early years, commercial television seemed to be answering the question more from a perspective of "what I want to be." The 1950s decade of programming was characterized by many in the field as an age of innocence and fantasy. What would later become public television fare was now commercial television. The Goodyear Playhouse, The Philco Playhouse, Shakespeare, and Children's Theatre were all part of TV.

Children were being programmed by age groups: weekday mornings and late afternoons for young children; early morning Saturdays for the very young with older children being entertained later in the morning. Sunday evenings were for families. There were two sides to this picture. On the one hand, children and their families were being generously, and even culturally, served. A magnetic and fascinating medium was picking up a lot of individual viewer time. Innocence had many dimensions, but among the most notable were the quality and the prevalence of children's programming and role models. In a time when Saturday morning programming itself was sparse, another mark of innocence was the relative absence of counterprogramming. Networks could concentrate on quality at any given Saturday morning hour and could simply not broadcast at other hours. Young television and even younger Saturday morning was being itself and still had a lot to learn.

By the 1960s, the playhouses were leaving prime time and the Howdys, the Winchells, and the Wizards were leaving Saturday morning. It was high-tide for cartoons and would remain so for most of the next three decades. A fallen innocence had begotten the science of counterprogramming, and with it the gravitational pull of ratings. It was a programming decade off to a rocky start with Newton Minow's "wasteland" label and ABC's "Bus Stop" shame. To attract young viewers, both the critics and the networks agreed ABC had been tasteless, paying the price of brutal competition for high ratings. There were calls for a roll-back in ratings emphasis but the profit-making roots went too deep for that. There was a call to exempt Saturday morning from the ratings tides, but the roots went too deep for that, too. The best of Saturday morning frequently was counterprogrammed, meaning that half of the best would not be seen and half of that best would die in the ratings competition.

For commercial television heading into the 1960s, Minow's "wasteland" label had cut deeply. The brief resurgence of fifties-style programming gave evidence of a hurt and uncertain medium struggling for respect. Comedy aided this struggle by virtually assuring high ratings while avoiding controversial issues. The specials concept presented a threat to regular series programming because it was relatively easy to "knock off" a given series' ratings with a top-billed special. Like going with the most experienced lineup on the crucial play, the specials era, as well as the cost of series programming, was ushering in conservatism and imitation. With the stakes riding on ratings, imitation was destined to continue and grow. Also destined to continue was the potential for another "Bus Stop." By the end of the sixties, there was mounting concern about the effect of TV on young viewers.

In the 1970s era, violence in programming and in advertising to children was coming to a head. Concern was expressed in the Surgeon General's Report early in the decade, and through consumer group effort and the Federal Trade Commission later in the decade. An indignant public wanted change and was taking major strides to get it. Once again, television was struggling for respectability and acceptance, getting little of either in a time of its own intensive self-reflection.

There were unintended misfortunes for children amid this turmoil. A prime-time access rule meant to spur creative local production efforts had instead created space for canned programming. A syndication company suit had aborted major new children's program initiatives at the networks. Family viewing time, well-intentioned and with public support, struck a First Amendment sandbar and died. Through all of this, television was caught between responsibility to its stockholders and responsibility to its public.

Atmospheres change and storms subside, revealing in their wake signs of destruction, promises of new growth, and even a somewhat-cleansed sameness. There was evidence of each of these in the decade of the eighties. Commercial television had made some concessions to its public (for example, host selling and reduced ad time per hour), while remaining true to its stockholders. It was even willing to help the Public Broadcasting System (PBS), partly out of selfishness, however. Perhaps TV's greatest mark of maturity was its willingness to address controversial topics and issues that previously would not have been aired, and were still considered risk-taking.

Saturday morning and children is indeed the television story. It reflects so much of the growing pains and the passages of commercial television itself. As Nielsen ratings competition escalated in prime time, it escalated in Saturday morning as well. As prime time was counterprogrammed, so was the best of Saturday morning. The excellence of a program became the excellence of its numbers. As the stakes grew higher, the trend was to imitate the success rather than to create, and the presold property became the children's program given. No one truly liked it, but everyone went by the numbers. As E.B. White said, it was "Excellence up to a point, but acceptability above all."[1] There was always excellence somewhere in children's programming, but it came more so in specials and drop-ins than in the regular schedule. And frequently the excellent in regular schedules was counterprogrammed.

Growing carries with it the challenge to blend realism and idealism without losing sight of either. We have seen many aspects of realism as they affect television and its Saturday morning. We will see many elements of the blend as we look toward the future.

Reference

1. Neil Hickey, "Public TV in Turmoil," *TV Guide* (July 23, 1977), p. 10.

12
Perspectives on the Future

I magine several diverse streams—some of them running parallel, others running at crosscurrents, none of them visible to the eye as they extend off into the distance. The future of commercial television programming for children resembles this picture. The end-point of existing streams is not yet discernible, but the reality of the streams themselves is quite vivid.

One of these realities—the emergence of foreign competition at the production and the technical levels—will have a major effect on children's future programming. In the production realm, a young company such as DIC may enjoy remarkable success in terms of network program buys. Whereas some of the larger companies are only getting continuation-type production, the young company picks up several new program buys. This pattern will have to be observed across several seasons to know whether it constitutes a prominent new impact on the production industry, but in the brief time DIC has been on the scene, its youthful management and program-development ideas have had a favorable reception at the networks.

Earlier we mentioned the network desire to have a relatively open market that includes new companies as well as established standards. Networks want the field to extend beyond the small handful monopoly of a few production companies. To the extent that new companies in the market are foreign-based entities such as DIC, the new entries may change the general profile of children's television production. In time, it is conceivable that the leading companies in terms of network buys will be European or Japanese-based firms, in some instances headed by an American executive, and in other instances, by European or Japanese ownership. If this scene emerges vividly, it would signal the passing of the torch in children's programming from early greats such as Hanna-Barbera to the new, foreign-based giants. As this torch is passed, a tone in children's programming undoubtedly will change. Program characteristics and lead roles will become more international in tone and in customs. Elements such as violence might take on an entirely different complexion, stemming directly from the cultural perception of violence in the production-based country. A Japanese tone, for instance, could bring with it more dramatically violent programming featuring the Sumarai depictions of violence effects, pain, and suffering. Program lead characters could become regular recipients of this violence, no longer having dramatic immunity by virtue of their lead character status. A program tone inevitably reflects its home production country.

Children's programming in this country might well reflect a reversal of what prime time and cartoon program exports have created in the past—an exporting of TV American values and a creation of worldwide fame and acceptance for American program and cartoon stars. To what extent the exporting process also has implanted American values into those cultural structures is impossible to measure. The extent to which the prospect of children's program importing will implant European or Japanese values in our cultural structures will be equally impossible to measure.

Beyond the prospect of program importing and values lies the economic reality of foreign-based companies. If they are able to effectively supply the American market at lower cost, they pose a lasting threat to the American-based children's production houses. The smaller production houses, already beleaguered and economically battered by their larger house counterparts, might now find it impossible to compete in an international marketplace. Lower labor costs and narrow profit margins could make it impossible for them to remain in business. The presence of the small production house, a creatively healthy entity in an already small market, would be lost.

The technical importing aspect resembles that which has occurred in several other industries. Regularly we buy merchandise with an American company name that is marked "Made in Japan" or "Made in Taiwan." The same is true for the children's production industry. Only one children's production company, Filmation, currently produces the animated program product from start to finish in this country. The more familiar scene is to ship the program elements abroad for animation work and final program assembly. Cost is the obvious benefit. This benefit is not without accompanying problems. Depending on an international plant halfway around the world for program shipment by new fall-season air date can be unsettling to producers and programming executives. It is equally unsettling to standards executives who may have little or no time with rough cut and will find any changes prior to air date impossible. Communications gaps via distance could mean the program received is a notably different translation from that intended within the elements sent. And an American production house work-force, experiencing heavy lay-offs in peak production season, will gradually move into other areas of the American work force, losing this concentration of technical expertise on the American scene.

Even without the element of foreign competition, production houses have found their three-buyer market too restrictive. There is always a thought about expanding markets and an eye toward discovering ways to accomplish this. Syndication is an obvious and current avenue. Hanna-Barbera, for instance, might syndicate sixty-five half-hour programs of the "Flintstones" and sell them to a group of television stations. Obviously, the more established houses, such as Hanna-Barbera and Filmation, have the greatest prospects for syndication. Their years and program credits give them a large program library ready for syndication. And they regularly review their "Hall of Fame" for prospects of creating original programs in one of their well-known series. The "Jetsons" and "Flintstones" have been recent examples of this type of production decision. Producing network or syndication specials within a well-known series also forms part of this diversification process.

Within the production community, there also has been the growing realization that network television reaches a substantially lower percentage of child viewers than in the past. Where Saturday morning viewing figures for network televison once ran in the range of 95 percent, the current figure typically is 60–65 percent. Producers are therefore prompted to ask a perfectly logical question, "Where are the other children viewing, and how could we reach them?" The answer to these questions is not a singular one, but we will consider the several viewer outlets that shape this general picture.

Cable Television

Some producers predict that cable will eventually have all children's television programming. The rationale for this prediction is the diminishing child viewership on the networks and the increasingly difficult challenge the networks have had in making their children's programming dollars cost-effective. Some would see a counterpart to the Disney channel concept as viable and on the near horizon. Larger production houses with a track record in this children's cast of characters would greatly benefit from this type of cable development. Nickelodean is the current version of that cable television prospect, and a Disney-type channel likely would feature more original work with familiar animation characters.

Videocassette

As the videocassette technology continues to spread within American homes and daily consciousness, production houses look toward the prospect of producing and selling children's program cassettes. This market began with Filmation's "He Man Masters of the Universe" cassette, but the retail price of that item ($25) limited the early market. Filmation plans greater volume at reduced cost, eventually targeting an original program videocassette for retail at $10 or less. Not only will this be a new outlet for production houses, but it will introduce a new flexibility into children's program viewing. How extensive and how large this market becomes will depend on a combination of price and consumer acceptance. Early indications of the latter would suggest it to be a fertile, untapped field.

International Satellite Transmission

On the current scene this thought is the most remote, and perhaps at the same time the most creative. It acknowledges that satellite transmission has made the world notably smaller, and suggests that this technology would enable a production house to do cartoons from other nations for worldwide distribution. Original cartoon work within foreign countries, building on the country's own richness of culture, heritage, and folklore, could be a deep and lasting treasure to children everywhere—one which may well bring with it the benefits of a heightened international awareness and mutual understanding. Until now, perhaps the closest approximation to this vision has been "Sesame Street" as it traveled "round the world" in various countries and translations. But even here the transmission was, in a sense, one-way. It would be exciting to envision the culture of a country joining forces with production house expertise for program sharing with the rest of the world. The vision is there as is the technology.

The future potential may be propelled toward more immediate reality as production houses find network markets shrinking. Always producers have felt the smallness. They will feel the shrinkage even more. And their quest for survival and a future will call on the depths of their creative imaginations and their perseverance.

To some extent, the future is endangered by its present. When a market is shrinking, gifted young people will pass it up as a professional option in favor of other, more promising avenues. At that point not only is the market shrinking, but the creative talent resource is shrinking as well. No one is more aware of this danger than the producers themselves. In the words of one creative production company head:

> Children's programming continues to be vulnerable. It has not grown. This is where I really look to broadcasters for their support to keep our area going. We can't get the exposure . . . they can.

> Children's programming has been seen in the industry as a second-class citizen. The territory is not glamorous. It's a stepping stone for a lot of executives. Network executives have to fight for franchises . . . after-school specials, and so forth . . . they have to fight to keep all those franchises alive. It's not a big money maker. It continues to be vulnerable.

Faced with the prospect of a shrinking creative talent resource, the production houses consciously encourage new talent:

> I'm going beyond bringing in writers to bringing in strictly idea people. I encourage them like a brain trust to create ideas which are new and fresh.

Yet smallness breeds its own "Catch 22" for creativity and growth. On the one hand, smallness means there is not as much money and incentive in children's programming as there is in prime time, and this reduces the likelihood of young creative talent choosing it as a career field. On the other hand, producers themselves like to keep it small. As long as children's programming remains limited and small, the opportunities for those currently within it are enhanced. Therefore, encouraging new talent and creativity runs headlong into "let's keep it small," making it difficult to maintain a productive balance.

There are several scenes emerging in the futuristic picture. In one scene, we see a small production village, prizing its smallness and applauding creativity. Like the suggestion of new development in a long-established neighborhood, its residents object to the change in its traditions, and in the atmosphere and opportunities. It is a village that gained its reputation on the grounds of its creativity and now wishes to retain the smallness of that heritage. Can it remain small yet vibrant and creative? What entree will it give to the young, creative talent? Whether this scene will be a success is not yet clear.

Producers wish to have their craft continue. The producer village cannot afford to choke out new talent, nor does it have the basic components for notable expansion. Likely it will remain small but not enclosed. New talent will be identified, apprenticed, and encouraged, and those possessing the new talent may see this village as a place they want to stay or as a great place to learn and then move on. It may become increasingly clear to these young people that the craft shops in which they have apprenticed are ill-equipped to compete in the international marketplace.

No village truly exists in isolation, and the children's television programming village is no exception. As the import market expands, there will be increasing numbers of European, Japanese, and other production houses springing up within the village. The production/writing community will become increasingly international in flavor and tone, much as the broadcast standards community has become today. More thought will be given to other countries, cultures, and customs, and the basic economic decisions on given production projects will become foreign-based rather than domestic. It is conceivable that some of the existing shops in the village, long-established firms with American work forces and strong reputations, will be bought by foreign-based companies. Although the base of creative talent and experience may not notably change in the early stages, the decision-making base will shift. The shift could be one of substance as well as tone.

Another possible village scene could find U.S. craft shops boarded up and for sale because their lack of flexibility and resilience amid changing markets and consumer trends rendered them unable to compete in a rapidly changing, high-technology environment. Colorful exhibits in major metropolitan museums would honor some of the shops and their notable accomplishments—an era revered and admired, yet past.

A brighter rendering of the village scene would find its craft shops bustling with young apprentices working alongside their foreign-shop counterparts. Change clearly will occur in their ways of thinking and their approach to children's program production, but it is a two-way process in which both the United States and its foreign-shop neighbors grow from their neighbor interaction. Identities are not lost. The American heritage shops retain their roots and the foreign-based shops retain theirs as well, but dialog is open and ongoing in an atmosphere that is refreshing and healthy. The combination of elements necessary to create this scene are intricately challenging. In addition to creativity, there is a commitment to dialogue and an open exchange of ideas in a competitive marketplace. This may be too much to ask, but it is not too much to hope.

Appendix A:
Interview Format for Producers

1. How long have you been in the television industry?
   a) How did you get your start?
   b) At what point did you become a producer?
   c) Do you see this as your career ambition, or is there something you would like to do beyond your current work? If so, what?

2. Tell me just a bit about your own background.
   a) Was producing always an ambition of yours or did it come later on?
   b) What was your dad's occupation and schooling?
   c) I'm told the definition of a native Californian is the first one off the plane. Were you raised here? (If applicable,) what brought you to LA initially?
   d) What would you tell a H.S. graduate he or she could expect, trying to enter the industry with hopes of becoming a producer? What could he or she anticipate in terms of rewards, difficulties, etc.?
   e) Would they be helped by any courses in child psychology or child development?
   f) Did you have any opportunity for courses like that in your own educational experience?
   g) To a young person interested in becoming a producer, would you recommend it enthusiastically as a career option? What is it about the business that would lead to your recommending enthusiastically or not recommending?

3. You've just been through a season of network "buys" for next fall.
   a) Describe the type of buys they made. What were they looking for this year?
   b) How would you rate their buys? Do you think they made the best choices, or could they have done better?
   c) How well did they match program interests your production house has had?

4. In effect, who determines the content of Saturday morning television?

5. What acts as the primary springboard for the program ideas you submit to the networks

6. How do you decide to what network you will submit a given idea?

7. How do you know in any given season what the networks are looking for? How do they spread that word, so to speak?

8. Once a children's program idea has been initiated, what path will it follow to the point of a "buy"? What are the critical points along that path?

9. Who will be weighing the potential of your program idea? What criteria will be entering into that weighing process?

10. Would you characterize the process as television-by-group or television-by-individual? (i.e., Is it primarily an individual or a group decision?)

11. How many ideas do you estimate you submit to the network for every idea
    a) you have accepted?
    b) that becomes a pilot?
    c) that becomes a series?
    d) that becomes a lasting series?

12. How do you gain access to children's opinions? What role do they have in the selection process?

13. What role does child development literature or child research play in the selection process?

14. What differences are there in the way the networks treat the large production houses and the small independents?
    a) Is the large production house more likely to get program ideas from the networks?
    b) If so, how does that affect the way the smaller independents interact with the networks?

15. Do networks deal with a limited number of producers? What criteria would a producer have to meet to have the confidence of a network?

16. What do you see as the strengths and weaknesses of the current program selection process? What recommendations would you make for improving it?

17. There seem to be ebbs and flows in the creative process in children's programming. Where one time period might be characterized as a witty, humor-oriented era, another might be described as more of a blam-blam, beat-their-brains-out era.
    a) How would you describe the themes in the current era?
    b) How do they differ from themes which immediately preceded them?
    c) What formula-type themes occur in virtually any era?

18. What group would spearhead change in children's television program content and themes?
    a) production studios?
    b) networks?
    c) children?
    d) general public?
    e) sponsors?
    f) political action or special interest groups?
    g) some other group or combination?

19. It has been said that "All television is educational television . . . ."
    a) What do you think the programs you write/produce are teaching?
    b) What do you wish they were teaching?
    c) Do you see yourself as a teacher when you write or produce? Why or why not?

20. Imagine for a moment that you have no constraints or limitations upon you at all, and that you can write/produce for children anything you wish.
    a) What would your program be?
    b) What key messages would it have?

21. Of all the children's series or specials you have worked on, what came closest to your ideal children's show? What was it about that show that especially appealed to you?

22. The comment has been made that in certain children's program eras "networks were telling producers how to produce, writers how to write, directors how to direct."
    a) To what extent do you feel that quote is true currently?

    b) How much freedom do you feel you have to be creative in your writing/producing?

    c) How would you describe your relationship with the networks?

    d) Do you feel that the networks see you primarily as artist, craftsman, servant, other?

23. Some believe the commercial programming field makes it difficult for producers and writers to realize many of their artistic and ethical values.

    a) To what extent do you think that statement is valid or true?

    b) What aspects of the production/writing atmosphere might prompt that kind of statement?

24. Which of the following groups do you have uppermost in mind when you write/produce?

    a) professional/artistic colleagues?

    b) buying organization (i.e., network, advertiser)?

    c) viewing audience?

    d) other?

25. Where do you get your conception of your audience?

    a) ratings of shows currently in the market?

    b) direct contact with children and their parents?

    c) your own personal impressions?

    d) child development literature?

    e) other?

26. Sketch briefly for me a word picture of the typical child viewer.

    a) age, sex, family setting

    b) social class

    c) personality characteristics, likes, dislikes, etc.

27. Given the fact that a new generation of viewers happens every three or four years, what impetus is there for new children's programming at all? Why not simply recycle?

28. What unwritten but generally understood laws have you found in the writing/producing business?

    a) What would a producer want to be sure to do?

    b) What would a producer want to be sure not to do?

29. You have a very extensive, unique, invaluable perspective on children's television programming . . . its ebbs, its flows, its change.

a) Thinking back and reflecting, how would you characterize the change you've seen over the years?
b) What changes would you foresee in children's television programming over the next five years? ten years?
c) How would you characterize children's television programming's current "state of health"?

Appendix B:
Interview Format for
Network Executives
(Children's Programming)

1. How long have you been in the television industry?
   a) How did you get your start?
   b) At what point did you become a network executive?
   c) Do you see this as your career ambition, or is there something you would like to do beyond your current work?

2. Tell me just a bit about your own background.
   a) Was working for a network always an ambition of yours or did it come later on?
   b) (d) What would you tell a H.S. or college graduate he or she could expect, trying to enter the business with hopes of working for a network? What could he or she anticipate in terms of rewards, difficulties, etc.?
   c) (e) Would they be helped by any courses in child psychology or child development?
   d) (f) Did you have any opportunity for courses like that in your own educational experience?
   e) (g) To a young person interested in becoming a network executive for children's programming, would you recommend it enthusiastically as a career option? What is it about the business that would lead to your recommending enthusiastically or not recommending?

3. You've just been through a season of program "buys" for next fall.
   a) Describe the type of buys you made. What were you looking for this year?
   b) How would you rate the production house ideas that came to you this year? Were you favorably impressed by their quality or did you feel they could have done better?
   c) How well did they match the program interests you had?

4   (5). What acts as the primary springboard for the program ideas submitted to you by production houses?

5   (8). Once a children's program idea has been presented to you, what path will it follow to the point of a "buy"? What are the critical points along that path?

6   (10). Would you characterize the process as television-by-group or television-by-individual? (i.e., Is it primarily an individual or a group decision?)

7.   How do you know what you want in Saturday morning programming for any given upcoming season?

8.   Who within the network makes that determination?

9   (13). What role does child development literature or child research play in the selection process?

10   (14). What differences are there in the way you treat the large production houses and the small independents?
   a) Is the large production house more likely to get program ideas from you?
   b) If so, how does that affect the way the smaller independents interact with you?

11   (15). What criteria would a producer have to meet to have the confidence of your network?

12   (16). What do you see as the strengths and weaknesses of the current program selection process? What recommendations would you make for improving it?

13   (17). There seem to be ebbs and flows in the creative process in children's programming. Where one time period might be characterized as a witty, humor-oriented era, another might be described as more of a blam-blam, beat-their-brains-out era.
   a) How would you describe the themes in the current era?
   b) How do they differ from themes which immediately preceded them?
   c) What formula-type themes occur in virtually any era?

14 (18). What group would spearhead change in children's television program content and themes?
  a) production studios?
  b) networks?
  c) children?
  d) general public?
  e) sponsors?
  f) political action or special interest groups?
  g) some other group or combination?

15 (19). It has been said that "All television is educational television . . . ."
  a) What do you think the programs you air are teaching?
  b) What do you wish they were teaching?
  c) Do you see yourself as a teacher when you select programming?

16 (20). Imagine for a moment that you have no constraints or limitations upon you at all, and that you can create any program you wish for children.
  a) What would your program be?
  b) What key messages would it have?

17 (21). Of all the children's series or specials you have worked on, what came closest to your ideal children's show? What was it about that show that especially appealed to you?

18 (22). The comment has been made that in certain children's program eras "networks were telling producers how to produce, writers how to write, directors how to direct."
  a) To what extent do you feel that quote is true currently?
  b) How much freedom do you feel producers have to be creative in their work?
  c) How would you describe your relationship with the producers?
  d) Do you see producers primarily as artists, craftsmen, servants, suppliers, or some other role characterization?
  e) In what role would you imagine producers feel they are seen by you?
  f) How do you think producers see you?

19 (29). You have a very extensive, unique, invaluable perspective on children's television programming . . . its ebbs, its flows, its change.

a) Thinking back and reflecting, how would you characterize the change you've seen over the years?

b) What changes would you foresee in children's television programming over the next five years? ten years?

c) How would you characterize children's television programming's current "state of health"?

Appendix C:
Interview Format for Network
Broadcast Standards Executives

1. How long have you been in the television industry?
   a) (1c) Do you see this as your career ambition, or is there something you would like to do beyond your current work?
   b) (2a) Was working for a network always am ambition of yours or did it come later on?
   c) (2e) Would a young person interested in working with broadcast standards at a network be helped by any courses in child psychology or child development?
   d) (2f) Did you have any opportunity for courses like that in your own educational experience?

2. You've just been through a season of program "buys" for next fall.
   a) (3b) From a broadcast standards perspective, how impressed were you with the production house ideas that came to the network this year? Were they relatively clean or did they need considerable work to meet broadcast standards?
   b) (3c) How does the production house know the broadcast standards criteria that will be applied to their program idea?

3. Do different production houses gain reputations within the review process—that if it came from X production house we'll have to review more closely than if it came from Y? Does that type of difference affect the program selection process itself (i.e., a great idea from House X would be put on a par with a good idea from House Y because House Y ideas traditionally require massive, close standards review and changes)?

4. A children's program idea has been presented to your network. There is network interest and a program development option to create the bible and some of the artwork.

    a) Where in this process will broadcast standards review be involved?

    b) Describe the nature of that involvement from the program option stage to the point of series buy.

    c) Do you review in tandem with children's programming or is your involvement totally independent of theirs?

    d) What are the critical review points along that program idea path?

5. Would you characterize the standards review process as group review or individual review? (10)

6 (13). What role does child development literature or child research play in the review process?

7. Do certain types of programs (e.g., maybe action/adventure) pose more review problems than others?

8 (10). What do you see as the strengths and weaknesses of the current program review process? What recommendations would you make for improving it?

9 (20). Imagine for a moment that you have no review constraints or limitations upon you at all, and that you can accept for children any program you wish.

    a) What would your program be?

    b) What key messages would it have?

10 (21). Of all the children's series or specials you have reviewed, what came closest to your ideal children's show? What about that show especially appealed to you?

12 (22). The comment has been made that in certain children's program eras "networks were telling producers how to produce, writers how to write, directors how to direct."

    a) To what extent do you feel that quote is true currently?

    b) How much freedom do you feel producers have to be creative in their work?

    c) How would you describe your relationship with the producers?

    d) How do you think producers see you?

e) In what role would you imagine producers feel they are seen by you?

f) Do you see producers more so as artists, craftsmen, servants, suppliers, or some other role characterization?

13 (29). a) Thinking back and reflecting, how would you characterize the change in children's programming broadcast standards you have seen over the years?

b) What changes would you foresee in broadcast standards for children's television programming over the next five years? ten years?

c) In terms of broadcast standards, how would you characterize children's television programming's current "state of health"? Would you like to see fewer standards or more standards?

14 (20). What do you find to be the most rewarding aspect of your position?

15 (21). What do you find to be its greatest frustration?

16 (22). What do you see as your greatest challenge?

17 (23). What effect do you think the network/review process has upon originality and creativity within the production houses?

18. The comment has been made that some of the world's finest children's literature has had significant, violent elements and that to remove those elements would be to neuter or to destroy the artistic creativity of the work itself. How would you respond to that type comment?

19. What do you see as meaningful steps that could be taken to ease the strain sometimes felt in the producer/network relationship?

Index